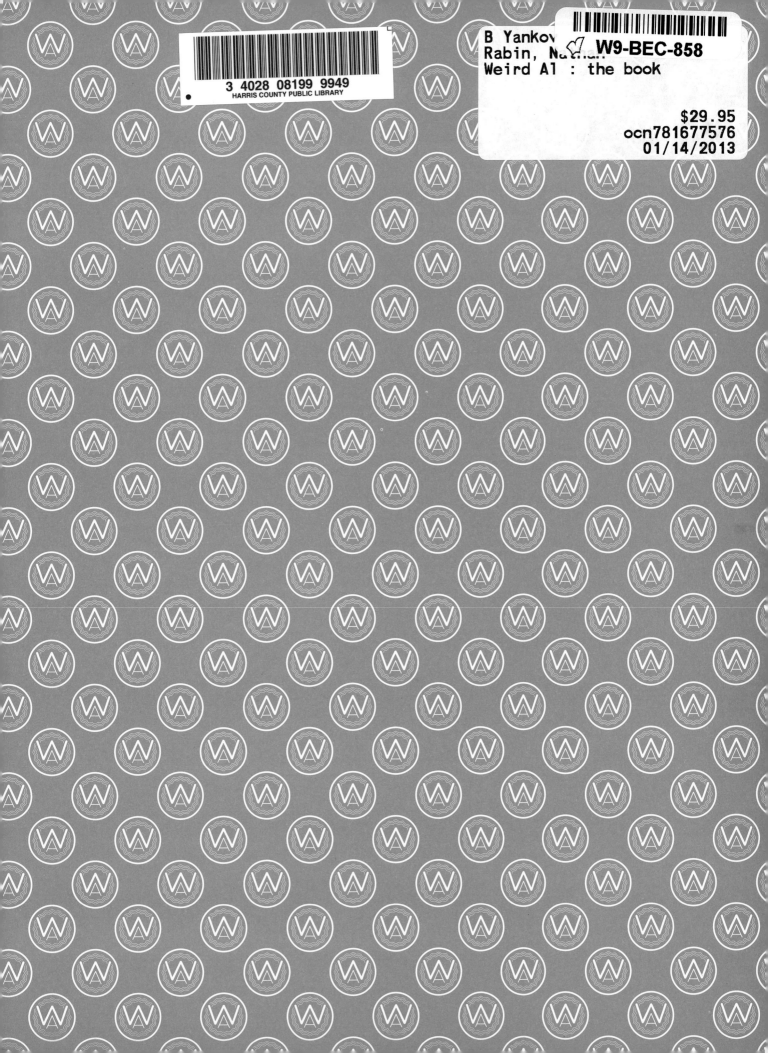

WEIRD AL

The Book

WEIRD AL

The Book

NATHAN RABIN
With AL YANKOVIC

Special Consultant: JON "BERMUDA" SCHWARTZ

ABRAMS IMAGE, NEW YORK

ACKNOWLEDGMENTS

If you had told my eleven-year-old self that he would one day write a book with his hero "Weird Al" Yankovic,
I suspect his fragile mind would have exploded from excitement and anticipation. The thirty-five-year-old
me was only slightly less exhilarated to get this assignment. So I would very much like to thank Al for having
the questionable judgment and considerable kindness to hire me, and for being so generous with his time,
recollections, and praise. I'd also like to thank him for having led such an incredible, eventful life that it made
my job easy. I'd like to thank Jay Levey and, especially, Jon "Bermuda" Schwartz, drummer extraordinaire
and the world's foremost expert on all things Al. This project wouldn't have been possible without you
and your obsessive archiving. I just hope I did justice to all that you, Al, his organization and band have
accomplished over the years. I am forever indebted to my agent Daniel Greenberg and to Brant Rumble,
who was kind enough to give me the go-ahead to work on this book, as well as the fine folks over at *A.V. Club*,
particularly Keith Phipps, Josh Modell, Scott Tobias, and Tasha Robinson. David Cashion, it was a pleasure
working with you and the good folks over at Abrams Image. Thanks for doing such a bang-up job on this
book—it's super pretty. Props go out to Michelle Welch for transcribing, and to my good friend Matt Lurie for
providing excellent company and a couch to crash on during my time in L.A. I would be nothing without my
bashert, Danya, who was there for me throughout the craziness of writing two books simultaneously without
taking time off from *The A.V. Club*. You are my everything. Dad, thanks for buying me Weird Al tapes when
I was a kid and for taking me to see Al for my very first concert. Lastly, I'd like to thank Al fans everywhere:
You are among the most passionate, committed, and loyal in existence, and I hope this book honors you and
your intense relationship with the greatest parody artist the world has ever known.

—Nathan Rabin

Editor: David Cashion
Art Direction: Headcase Design
Designer: Danielle Young
Production Manager: Ankur Ghosh

Library of Congress Cataloging-in-Publication Data

Rabin, Nathan, 1976-
  Weird Al : the book / Nathan Rabin ; introduction by "Weird Al"
Yankovic.
    p. cm.
  ISBN 978-1-4197-0435-2
1. Yankovic, Al, 1959- 2. Accordionists—United States—Biography. 3.
Rock musicians—United States—Biography. 4. Parody in music.
I. Title.
  ML419.Y35R33 2012
  792.7'6092—dc23
  [B]
                    2012020735

Text and compilation copyright © 2012 Al Yankovic

Published in 2012 by Abrams Image, an imprint of ABRAMS.

Printed and bound in China
10 9 8 7 6 5 4 3 2 1

Abrams Image books are available at special discounts
when purchased in quantity for premiums and promotions
as well as fundraising or educational use. Special editions
can also be created to specification. For details, contact
specialsales@abramsbooks.com or the address below.

115 West 18th Street
New York, NY 10011
www.abramsbooks.com

★ CONTENTS ★

INTRODUCTION—by Al Yankovic ★ 6

CHAPTER 1

PORTRAIT OF THE PARODY ARTIST AS A YOUNG MAN
★ 8 ★

CHAPTER 2

THE EAT IT GUY
★ 44 ★

CHAPTER 3

KURT COBAIN SAVES ROCK & ROLL AND ALSO AL'S CAREER
★ 102 ★

CHAPTER 4

A NEW LOOK AL FOR A NEW ERA
★ 140 ★

CHAPTER 5

THE ALPOCALYPSE APPROACHES
★ 168 ★

DISCOGRAPHY ★ 202

VIDEOGRAPHY ★ 205

PHOTO CREDITS ★ 208

INTRODUCTION

By Al Yankovic

WELCOME TO *WEIRD AL: THE BOOK*. CATCHY TITLE, RIGHT? BOLD, SIMPLE . . . PRETTY MUCH SAYS EVERYTHING IT NEEDS TO SAY. ORIGINALLY I WANTED TO CALL IT *A BRIEF HISTORY OF TIME*, BUT I WAS INFORMED THAT TITLE HAD ALREADY BEEN TAKEN. OH WELL.

Here's the thing—I always thought it would be cool to have my own large-format coffee-table-style book, but I never had any interest at all in writing an autobiography. I've done the *Behind the Music*s, the *Biography* shows . . . I've done a brain-melting number of TV appearances, radio interviews, and podcasts over the years . . . Frankly, I just don't have anything else to say about myself! Most of my semi-amusing anecdotes have become nauseatingly familiar to my hard-core fans. I'm not holding back any deep, dark secrets. Plus, 97 percent of celebrity autobiographies seem to devolve into pathetic navel-gazing—I didn't like my odds.

So, I asked Abrams Books to hire Nathan Rabin to do the heavy lifting. I'd always been a huge fan of *The Onion*, and always admired Nathan's work (he was—and is—the head writer of their A.V. Club). I also enjoyed reading his memoir *The Big Rewind* . . . In fact, what probably sealed the deal for me was the fact that Nathan had thanked me in the back of his book, in return for (as he explained to me later) keeping him somewhat sane during a troubled adolescence. I took this as a sign. As a wise man once said (or probably *should* have), "If you're going to hire somebody to write a book about you, it's always a good idea to choose somebody who doesn't think you *suck*."

Nathan did a phenomenal job—and he certainly saved me the grueling task of having to personally write hundreds of pages about my own sheer *awesomeness*. If I did *that*, how would you know how incredibly *humble* I really am?

I also have to give an enormous amount of credit to my faithful drummer of more than thirty years, Jon "Bermuda" Schwartz, who was an integral part of putting this book together. Bermuda, because of his loveably obsessive ways, is the de facto archivist of all things Weird Al. He's our biggest fan. I'm kind of hoping that I die before he does, because he's threatened that if *he* goes first, I'm going to wind up with all of his crap. Anyway, Jon went through tens of thousands of photos during this process, and he managed to dig up some real treasures.

Of course, I want to thank the fans who contributed their own photos to this book, made amazing pieces of art, permanently scarred their flesh with my image, or were just generally supportive of me doing what I do. I really and truly appreciate it.

And most of all, I want to thank . . . me. I think it's pretty obvious that without me, this book would be severely lacking in subject matter. Also, I wound up doing a fair amount of "special material" for the book, including all the captions for the photographs, ten ridiculous lists of random things, thirty-eight of my favorite tweets, the lyrics from my most popular songs, and the introduction that—I have to assume—you are *reading right now*.

We all had a lot of fun making this book. Hope you enjoy it!

CHAPTER 1

PORTRAIT

of the

PARODY

ARTIST

as a

YOUNG MAN

★ Even as a toddler, I embraced the Hollywood lifestyle.

ALFRED MATTHEW YANKOVIC OF LYNWOOD, CALIFORNIA, GRADU-
ATED VALEDICTORIAN OF HIS HIGH SCHOOL CLASS AT AGE SIXTEEN
IN 1975, BUT HIS REAL EDUCATION CAME FROM *MAD* MAGAZINE.

MAD showed children the way the world really worked. Yankovic's early education in *MAD* was later augmented by graduate studies in the madcap offerings of eccentric musical geniuses like Spike Jones, Stan Freberg, Frank Zappa, Allan Sherman, Shel Silverstein, and Tom Lehrer courtesy of a brilliant, idiosyncratic musicologist born Barry Hansen but known to the world as Dr. Demento.

These strange, disproportionately bespectacled satirists saw through the ridiculous charade of pop music—a preposterous realm where lovers were invariably romantic, well-groomed, and nonpsychotic, holidays were a source of joy instead of trauma, and Santa Claus abstained from perpetrating Yuletide bloodbaths.

The man the world would come to know as "Weird Al" Yankovic wouldn't follow any of those rules. In his songs, love manifests itself as an ugly and destructive form of mental illness, holidays are to be endured, and Santa Claus has a body count.

Yankovic's comic elders were preparing him for a unique destiny. The future icon would become to pop music what *MAD* is to our culture as a whole: its preeminent satirist.

Weird Al was never supposed to last. A glowing review of *"Weird Al" Yankovic in 3-D*, his second studio album, accidentally made that point when it breathlessly praised Yankovic for his surprising longevity and consistency—in 1984. Who could have imagined that almost three decades later Yankovic would be bigger than ever? Yankovic has mastered the art of the loving parody, the spoof that betrays its creator's profound affection for what he's satirizing. Yankovic is such a genial and affable cultural commentator that it can be easy to overlook his oeuvre's sustained and quietly provocative

★ Nick and Mary Yankovic (a.k.a. Dad and Mom).

thousand-inch television so massive it allows him to watch *The Simpsons* from thirty blocks away, it sounds ridiculous because it *is* ridiculous. But it also sounds glorious. Yankovic's parodies almost invariably come from a place of affection and respect (assuming you're not Billy Ray Cyrus).

For nearly thirty years, Al has occupied a privileged place in pop culture as our unofficial official musical satirist, but few could have predicted all that would transpire from Yankovic's humble beginnings.

Alfred was born on October 23, 1959 to Nick and Mary Yankovic of lower-middle-class Lynwood, California, just north of a suburb familiar to music fans for a much different reason: N.W.A.'s infamous Compton. Nick Yankovic had won a Silver Star (and two Purple Hearts) for his heroics as a medic in World War II. Without the advantage of a high school education, the elder Yankovic had served as a makeshift doctor on the battlefield, but upon his return home he meandered professionally before ultimately enjoying a long stint at a steel manufacturing plant. He was a cheerful, gregarious man with a sometimes dark and morbid sense of humor that would prove a formative influence on his young son's personality.

Mary Yankovic was a stenographer who was always jotting down notes in some strange code young Alfred did not understand. Al's father was outgoing, a consummate people pleaser, while his mother was more reserved. Al would take after both of his parents. He inherited Nick's loquacious disposition and eagerness to entertain as well as Mary's underlying seriousness.

This proved to be a formidable combination that would eventually rocket Al Yankovic's career to great

satire of the rapaciousness and excess of the American consumer.

Yankovic subversively inhabits the avaricious minds of the reckless hedonists convinced that true happiness lies with the acquisition of a velvet Elvis painting or a transcendent trip to the hardware store or the perfect condo: contentment always has a price tag.

Yet within this send-up of consumerism lies a distinct note of appreciation. When Yankovic sings of a two-

TWEET

Sure, my neighbors can leave their Christmas lights up all year, yet they complain about me setting off fireworks every night. Sheesh!

★ Me, sitting on a beach ball . . . next to the beach ball's natural enemy, the floor heater.

heights. Through the years, the class clown and valedictorian would not only comfortably coexist within Al but also thrive. The class clown delighted in making a spectacle of himself. The valedictorian made sure Al had a solid backup plan, impeccable grades, and a practical degree in case his preposterous ambition to make a go of it recording silly songs for a living somehow didn't pan out.

Young Alfred was incredibly precocious. He began kindergarten a year early in 1963 and later skipped second grade, so he was generally two years younger than everyone in his class. Despite the age gap, Yankovic threw himself into his studies and extracurricular activities. In the National Forensic League, Yankovic excelled in "Humorous Interpretation" and "Expository Speaking" and he ultimately graduated valedictorian at sixteen.

Yankovic's other extracurricular activities presaged the surreal direction in which his life would be heading. Al's penchant for performing got him cast as a hood in a high school production based on *Rebel Without a Cause*.

If Yankovic's immortal turn as "Crunch," a hoodlum in the *Rebel*-inspired production, anticipated Al's career in the spotlight, his status as the founding member of his school's "Volcano Worshippers Club," an organization that existed solely so Al could sneak one more picture of himself into the school yearbook, betrayed his absurdist sense of humor—a smart-ass sensibility informed by Monty Python and *MAD* as well as his beloved musical mirth-makers.

Furthermore, young Alfred's parents had made a crucial decision. In a world where most children grow up learning how to play guitar or drums, Yankovic's parents decided to enroll their Al in accordion lessons that began on October 22, 1966, the day before his seventh birthday.

For lack of a better word, Yankovic's family had picked an instrument for their son that was *weird*. If the electric guitar is the ultimate rock-and-roll babe magnet, the accordion is its antithesis. Guitarists look amazing exerting the least possible effort. All they have to do is stand there and look devastatingly hip.

An accordion player, on the other hand, can just stand there and look agonizingly awkward. Guitars are so inher-

ently cool that people don't even have to play them to tap in to their iconic power; simply holding an acoustic guitar in your hands and looking thoughtful is enough to impress certain college coeds. An accordion player at the end of a long show, however, often looks less like a rock god than the Michelin Man in the midst of an asthma attack.

★ Is there anything cooler than a kid with an accordion? Besides everything else in the world?

A seven-year-old with an accordion is an instant sight gag. The instrument had become synonymous with bubble machines and beer-barrel polkas and Lawrence Welk. So when Yankovic decided to use his beloved LP of Elton John's *Goodbye Yellow Brick Road* to figure out how to play rock and roll on the accordion, the juxtaposition was inherently comic.

Without giving it much thought, Yankovic was already laying down the cornerstones of his future career. He was cobbling together a homemade aesthetic out of the

LITTLE KNOWN FACTS ABOUT ME

My social security number is 547-26-8624.

Sometimes when I'm at home and nobody else is around, I like to dress up in men's clothing.

I strongly believe that marriage should only be between a man and a multi-cellular life form.

When I'm performing, I never give 110%, because that's metaphysically impossible.

Once I toured for a year as Kenny G and nobody ever caught on.

squeeze box, his love of rock and pop culture, and his growing fascination with cracked, cerebral musical funnymen such as the aforementioned Lehrer, Freberg, Zappa, and Sherman. Yankovic's life could very well have followed a much different, much straighter path if his mother hadn't discovered that the local Pic 'N' Save was selling a huge number of albums for a quarter apiece, including plenty of Allan Sherman albums when Al was five or six.

Before he became an unlikely pop star, Yankovic was a devoted student of music and comedy. He was such a passionate student of comedy in particular that he would transcribe George Carlin albums word for word. Even at an early age, Yankovic was analyzing entertainment critically, taking it apart to see how it worked.

Young Alfred was an accidental deconstructionist; as an adult he would disassemble the songs of his favorite artists and reconstruct them in his own image for his pastiches. He would determine just what made a Devo song a Devo song or a Talking Heads song a Talking Heads song, then reassemble the parts into a new creation. Alfred was such a fan of Tom Lehrer that he actually contemplated enrolling at the University of California, Santa Cruz, where Lehrer was a math professor, just so that he could learn at the feet of a master before ultimately deciding to go to California Polytechnic State University to study architecture.

Yankovic was aching for another avenue to express himself. He found the perfect vehicle for his peculiar passions when he began listening to *The Dr. Demento Show* on the local Los Angeles radio station KMET in what Yankovic fuzzily recalls as 1971 or 1972.

Young Alfred was transfixed. Here was a show that spoke to him on a profound and profoundly silly level. *The Dr. Demento Show* was an audio funhouse, part radio, part musical vaudeville. Like Al, the show had a deep appreciation of musical and comedy history; Dr. Demento was less a traditional disc jockey than a warped music professor, and Al was to become his most distinguished student.

The Dr. Demento Show didn't just give young Alfred something to do with his free time. It gave him a whole

★ My high school senior picture. I would not date for several more years.

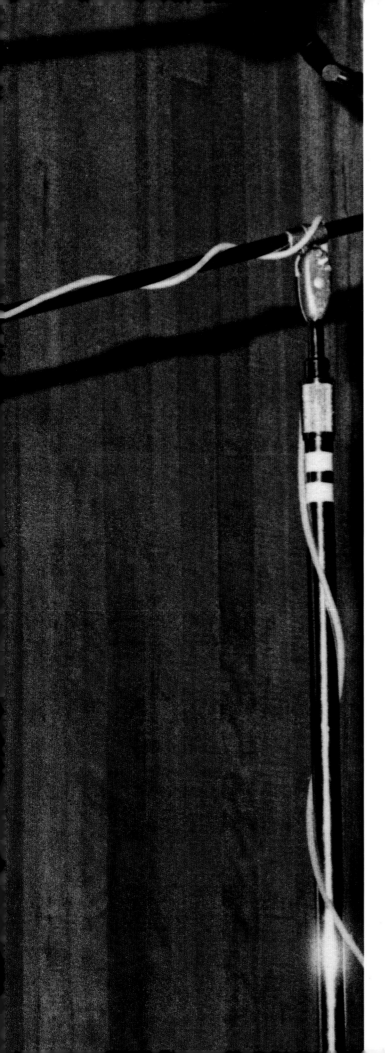

weird new world to get lost in, populated by eccentric, larger-than-life figures that were crazy or geniuses or both.

Demento would eventually become a mentor, a teacher, a guru, and a star-maker. But when Al discovered *The Dr. Demento Show* at age twelve or thirteen, he knew its host solely as a zany voice on his radio.

Barry Hansen, aka Dr. Demento, was a lot like Al Yankovic: a fundamentally serious, almost preternaturally informed student of music in the professional equivalent of a jester's costume. Hansen was a student of music in the most literal sense: he had a master's in folklore and ethnomusicology from UCLA. He was a jack-of-all-trades in the music business. He'd worked as a roadie, a freelance music historian and record reviewer, and he

★ On stage at my college campus coffee house. My show-stopping number was a medley of every song ever written in the history of the world (played on the accordion, of course).

★ My de-mentor, Dr. Demento.

at Pic 'N' Save and his parents' sagacious decision to have their son learn accordion instead of guitar, it was one of a series of fortuitous coincidences that would send Al's life and career spinning in strange and inspired directions. In his liner notes for *Permanent Record,* Yankovic's box set, Demento writes that the thirteen-year-old Al was too nervous to say much when he got the radio personality's autograph but he did make sure to hand him a cassette he'd made of himself and some friends performing "Pico and Sepulveda," the show's theme song, for a contest the show was running. Little did Demento realize the central role he would play in the young man's musical evolution.

Within the weird, wonderful world of Dr. Demento, the first meeting of "Weird Al" Yankovic and his mentor-to-be was a game-changer. It was the wacky-music equivalent of Brian Epstein discovering the Beatles. Demento was flattered by Yankovic's interest in him. Yankovic, meanwhile, was so self-conscious about his voice that he didn't even sing on his contest entry, which went nowhere.

Al was delighted when a song he submitted a few years later in 1976 to *The Dr. Demento Show* called "Belvedere Cruising" inexplicably emanated from his radio during the show. Al was also confused; he initially wondered if he'd accidentally set off his own 8-track player but was overjoyed to discover that his homemade ditty had made his favorite radio show. It had happened. A song Alfred Yankovic had written and recorded was being played on the radio. He'd made it. He would later say that he was more excited about hearing his song on *The Dr. Demento Show* than just about anything that's happened to him professionally since.

did A&R work for a small record label before finding his true calling hosting a two-hour-long all-novelty show that was syndicated nationwide by Al's future employers at Westwood One.

So you can only imagine Al's excitement when he learned that Dr. Demento would be coming to his very high school for an after-school assembly on music appreciation in 1973. Like the twenty-five-cent Allan Sherman albums

Nothing in the world makes you feel as worthless and insignificant as not finding your name at a souvenir license plate stand.

There's nothing novel about writing an ode to an automobile. The Beach Boys recorded dozens. But "Belvedere Cruising" was unlike anything Brian Wilson and the gang ever recorded: it was a tribute to the lumbering monstrosity that was Al's parents' big black 1964 Plymouth Belvedere with red upholstery. Even when young Alfred attacked what passed for standard rock-and-roll subject matter, he did so from an unexpected angle.

Al had experienced his first taste of professional success. It fueled his hunger. Yankovic began regularly submitting songs to the show. He was approaching his new sideline as a musical funnyman with the focus and determination that would rocket him to the pinnacle of his field.

In a bid to make *The Dr. Demento Show*'s fabled "Funny Five" countdown, Yankovic and his friends would bombard the show with requests for Yankovic's songs. Al engaged in blatant vote fixing but scheming wasn't just tolerated at *The Dr. Demento Show*; it was expected.

Nevertheless, in a typewritten letter dated August 19, 1976, Demento gently took his protégé to task for his all-out assault on his request line when he wrote, "I can take a certain degree of ballot-box-stuffing—but only so much. I've gotten just about 'so much' from Lynwood—perhaps just a little bit more than 'so much.'"

The avuncular Demento included constructive praise for his young protégé along with a gentle scolding. After a wry reference to Yankovic's antics being unfair to other aspiring artists without "petition machines," Demento closed the letter with the encouraging words "Please keep sending me your songs. I do believe you have the talent to create songs that will arouse support from those who don't go to school with you" and a closing admonition to "stay demented."

Demento's affection for the polite young man with the petition machine was evident, as was Yankovic's respect for Demento.

It would be hard to overstate the influence that *The Dr. Demento Show* (or *MAD* magazine) had on young Alfred. In college, he and best friend Joel Miller (who accompanied on bongos) would perform covers of songs they'd heard on the show along with the occasional origi-

nal like "Mr. Frump in the Iron Lung," a vaudeville-style number that found its way onto Al's first album. During his sophomore year of college, the alternately shy and attention-hungry geek with the accordion further refined his nascent persona as the host of his college radio's *Weird Al Show,* a collection of sketches, wacky call-in guests, and banter that aired during the graveyard shift. Al doesn't remember why the folks in his freshman dorm nicknamed him "Weird" but by the time he hosted his own radio show sophomore year, Weird Al had become his professional name.

Young Alfred found a home in *The Dr. Demento Show* and a teacher and mentor in its genially wacky host. On breaks from college, he would man the phones, premiere new songs, and hang out with some of the other colorful characters who populated the good doctor's world. Al was particularly fond of a multitalented young man named Art Barnes who, as half of the duo Barnes & Barnes, had one of *The Dr. Demento Show*'s signature

★ The night I debuted "Another One Rides the Bus" live on the air was preceded by a weekend camping trip with the Demento gang (L to R: "Beefalo Bill" Burk, "Ludicrous Lorri" O'Grady, Dr. D., *moi*, and Dan "Damaskas" Hollombe).

hits with "Fish Heads." As a *Lost in Space* fan, Al was impressed by Barnes's impressive collection of *Lost in Space* memorabilia. It wasn't until later that the usually sharp Yankovic realized that the man he knew under the stage name Art Barnes was actually Bill Mumy, the child star of *Lost in Space*.

★ Now a national monument (or at least it *should* be), this is the urinal in the bathroom across the hall from my campus radio station, KCPR—the site where I recorded the original version of "My Bologna."

While still an architecture student at Cal Poly, Al wrote a parody of the Knack's number one Billboard single "My Sharona" called "My Bologna" and recorded it in the bathroom of the college radio station. The song became a smash on *The Dr. Demento Show*, eventually hitting number one on the

Sept. 27, 1979

Hi Alfred   (would you rather I called
            you Al on the air ?)

much belated thanks for your wondrous
sausage music.

It has made a big hit with my
audience, to put it mildly.

It's been on my KMET Top Ten twice,
ditto for the Top Ten on my new show
on KSAN in San Francisco. On my
national show it will be #1 on the
show just taped for broadcast two weeks
from Sunday.

A producer from Capitol Records,
Bruce Ravid, called and asked for a
copy for The Knack.

You might want to send a copy to Harold
Bronson at Rhino Records, 11609 W. Pico,
Los Angeles, CA 90064. They have been
putting out a lot of comedy records
lately. Tell him I sent you.

Stay Demented !

Dr. Demento

Barry

★ When I got this letter from Dr. Demento saying that my song had topped
his "Funny Five" countdown for two weeks in a row, I really thought that
I had peaked. "Life can't possibly get any better than *this*!"

Executive and General Offices

December
14 th
1979

Mr. Alfred Yankovic
1025 Foothill Blvd. Apt. 19
San Luis Obispo, California 93401

Dear Al,

    Enclosed is our check number 497851 in the amount
of $500 as a recoupable advance against royalties re-
presenting full payment for two masters.

    Best regards.

               Very truly yours,

               Arnold J. Holland
               Director, Business Affairs

AJH:jg

Enclosure (check)

Page 10—San Luis Obispo County (Calif.) Telegram-Tribune Thursday, April 24, 1980

"Weird Al" Yankovic twirls dials at KCPR.

KCPR disc jockey hits the big time

By Alison Harvey
Staff Writer

Cal Poly's own Weird Al has hit the big time on the bizarre record circuit.

Weird Al (Alfred M. Yankovic), an architecture major, knocked on doors for years with his novelty songs and take-offs on hit rock recordings.

Capitol Records opened up for his version of the Knack's hit song, "My Sharona," which he titled "My Bologna."

Released last December, Yankovic's single sold about 10,000 copies in the first month.

It goes like this:

"Never going to stop,
Eat it up, such a tasty snack,
I always eat too much and throw up,
But I'll soon be back for
My, my, my yi, yi, yi, woo,
Ma, ma, ma, ma, my-y-y-y bologna."

Those lines made Yankovic, 20, a modest amount of pocket money, and even though the record hasn't sold "terribly well," it has made his name known in the novelty record business.

Dr. Demento, a Los Angeles area disc jockey with a show that features bizarre recordings got

(Continued in Page 11)

★ As you can see in this letter, I was paid a sum total of $500 for the masters to my single "My Bologna"—not a whole lot, but I *did* record it in a bathroom, after all. The punchline is—when I re-recorded the song for my first album with a different label, Capitol charged me $1,000 for the privilege. That, friends, is why it's called the record *business.*

Funny Five. In an almost suspiciously fortuitous sequence of events, the Knack played a show at Cal Poly. Afterward, Yankovic sheepishly introduced himself to Doug Fieger, the group's lead singer, as the man behind "My Bologna." Fieger had heard and dug the song, and quite literally turned around to Capitol Records vice president Rupert Perry, who happened to be standing there, and suggested that Capitol release the parody as a single.

Perry knew better than to doubt the judgment of the lead singer of the Knack, so he signed Yankovic to a six-month contract and paid $500 for the master to "My Bologna." On Christmas Eve 1979, Capitol Records, the legendary home of groups like the Beatles and the Beach Boys, released "My Bologna" with an obscure track called "School Cafeteria" as the B-side.

It was not the most glamorous of launches. A *Variety* blurb from Wednesday, December 12, hilariously quipped, "At Capitol, meanwhile, a new single is on its way by—seriously—

★ On stage with buddies Joel Miller (bongos) and Joe Earley (jaw harp) at a college event called Poly Royal. I'm not sure, but I think the kid in the foreground may have been our entire audience.

Wendell Yankovich. The tune—not too seriously, folks— is called **My Bologna,** based on you-know-what."

"Wendell Yankovich" had arrived. Or perhaps not. It was a surreal experience for Al, releasing a single on Capitol and having his songs played on the radio while at the same time trudging his way toward a degree in architecture he felt less excited about by the day. Al had accomplished much in his brief musical career—and when he searched his soul, he had to admit that he was never particularly enthusiastic about being an architect. It was the kind of mildly dispiriting day job/backup plan Al's high school guidance counselor had encouraged him to get after chiding him that his dream of making a living in comedy as a *MAD* writer and cartoonist was terribly unrealistic and that he would be better off pursuing a more practical career.

Yankovic did not realize it at the time, but one of the finalists in the "Pico and Sepulveda" contest he had entered back in high school would go on to play

ANOTHER ONE RIDES THE BUS

(OOH! LET'S GO!)

RIDIN' IN A BUS DOWN THE BOULEVARD
AND THE PLACE WAS PRETTY PACKED
I COULDN'T FIND A SEAT, SO I HAD TO STAND
WITH THE PERVERTS IN THE BACK
IT WAS SMELLIN' — LIKE A LOCKER ROOM
THERE WAS JUNK ALL OVER THE FLOOR
WE'RE ALREADY PACKED IN LIKE SARDINES
BUT WE'RE STOPPIN' TO PICK UP MORE— LOOKOUT!

CHORUS: ANOTHER ONE RIDES THE BUS
ANOTHER ONE RIDES THE BUS
AND ANOTHER COMES ON AND ANOTHER COMES ON
ANOTHER ONE RIDES THE BUS
HEY! HE'S GONNA SIT BY YOU
ANOTHER ONE RIDES THE BUS

THERE'S A SUITCASE POKIN' ME IN THE RIBS
THERE'S AN ELBOW IN MY EAR
THERE'S A SMELLY OLD BUM STANDIN' NEXT TO ME
HE HASN'T SHOWERED IN A YEAR
WELL, I THINK I'M MISSIN' A CONTACT LENS
I THINK MY WALLET'S GONE
AND I THINK THIS BUS IS STOPPIN' AGAIN
TO LET A COUPLE MORE FREAKS GET ON, ~~YEAH!~~ LOOKOUT!

(REPEAT CHORUS)
(INSTRUMENTAL WITH BUS SOUND EFFECTS AND DIALOGUE)

ANOTHER ONE RIDES THE BUS
ANOTHER ONE RIDES THE BUS, OW!
ANOTHER ONE RIDES THE BUS, HEY HEY!
ANOTHER ONE RIDES THE BUS, HEY-Y-Y-Y-Y!

OVER →

★ In the U.S., the "Another One Rides the Bus" single was shipped in a generic TK Records sleeve, but internationally it got a little more love, as evidenced by this Dutch release.

a huge role in his life and career. Drummer/percussionist Jon Schwartz met Yankovic on September 14, 1980, while the future superstar was practicing for a live performance of his latest song, a parody of Queen's "Another One Bites the Dust" titled "Another One Rides the Bus" on *The Dr. Demento Show*. Schwartz mentioned that he was a drummer and volunteered his services on the only percussive-type entity available: a beat-up accordion case. Weird Al would go on to give his drummer a weird nickname of his own when he dubbed him Jon "Bermuda" Schwartz.

★ Bermuda and I were pretty darn excited to fly out to New York and appear on Tom Snyder's *Tomorrow Coast to Coast*. It was our first national TV appearance ever. I wasn't particularly well known at the time—we were one of three "goofy novelty music" acts that were booked for this particular show.

In that moment, all young Alfred needed was someone to bang on his accordion case in rhythm. What he ended up with was an invaluable lifelong collaborator. Schwartz wouldn't just provide the rhythmic foundation for Yankovic's music, he would also serve as his unofficial photographer, archivist, personal historian, webmaster, and coffee-table-book consultant. Schwartz's obsessive tendencies are legendary. He has famously collected and preserved in his garage everything even tangentially related to Yankovic's career.

If Yankovic is the antithesis of the stereotypical

 **TWEET** Does anybody know the expiration on whoop-ass? I opened a can last week and I'm not sure if it's still good.

self-destructive rock star—a sober, clean-living, fiscally responsible, extraordinarily well-preserved consummate mensch with a pristine reputation—then Schwartz is similarly the antithesis of the stereotypical wild-man drummer.

The rock-and-roll drummer is supposed to be like Animal from *The Muppet Show*, only with fewer social graces: a crazy, flailing, hard-living, hard-partying, irresponsible maniac. He's supposed to be the lunatic who misses the gig because he's passed out in a ditch somewhere. Schwartz is the opposite. Within the world of Al, Schwartz is the freakishly well-organized, prepared, and methodical man who makes sure that everything proceeds smoothly.

For Al and his new drummer, that ad-hoc performance of "Another One Rides the Bus" would prove a

defining moment. The geek with the ferocious drive and his accordion-case beater were going to make an impression even if Yankovic had to blow out his nasal whine screaming his displeasure at the indignities of public transportation. And the primitive recording techniques and bare-bones instrumentation (just an accordion and a madman beating on an accordion case) were pure DIY.

Though the modest Yankovic himself laughs off the notion, we can now all agree that "Another One Rides the Bus" embodies the anarchic spirit of punk rock just as much as anything Johnny Rotten or the Clash ever recorded. It's the essence of punk: an enraged, defiant malcontent with a long list of grievances screaming his pain to an indifferent world.

★ My last "day job"—working in the mail-room for the radio syndication company Westwood One. I gave my notice the morning I picked up the mail and noticed that I was on *Billboard's* Hot 100 list.

In the best punk tradition, "Another One Rides the Bus" is all about attitude, energy, and volume. It's a triumph of youthful brattiness over craft, polish, and professionalism—a homemade howl of rage. Yankovic came to symbolize a curiously ubiquitous fixture of new wave: the enraged geek.

Al was graduating from college all right, but his passion lay with music, not architecture. "My Bologna" and "Another One Rides the Bus" had taken Al and his drum-mer/co-conspirator exciting places. "My Bologna" made him a major-label recording artist, however short-lived, and the popularity and airplay of "Another One Rides the Bus" won Al and Jon an invitation to perform the song on Tom Snyder's *The Tomorrow Show.*

Nothing in Snyder's exquisitely condescending intro-duction of Yankovic suggested the energetic young man anxiously clutching the squeeze box would be around for three more months, let alone three more decades. Snyder couldn't even be bothered to recall the name of the song Yankovic would be performing, leaving Al to helpfully chip in that he and Schwartz would be favoring audiences with "Another One Rides the Bus." In his TV debut, Al is all nervous, flailing energy as he bashes his way through the song, his hair a mop of frizz, his skinny limbs flying. Bare-foot and clad in quilted velvet pants, Yankovic looked as crazy as he sounded. Schwartz, meanwhile, conveyed an incongruous dignity as he bashed on the fabled accordion case and worked various sound effects. Al had never been to New York before. Now he was experiencing it in the most intensely nerve-wracking manner imaginable. It was terrifying and exhilarating in equal measure.

It was a rush flying to New York to perform on na-tional television. With each passing day, Al's enthusiasm for architecture faded and his love of performing grew.

After graduation, Al decided to spend a few years pursuing a record deal. He applied for jobs everywhere but architectural firms and eventually landed a job in the mailroom at radio syndication giant Westwood One.

Al was doing menial work, delivering mail and taking out trash, but he was in the industry. Yankovic's double life as a parody-superstar-in-the-making and a wage slave at

I have to assume that "got your nose!" game got really old with Voldemort after a while.

★ Going indie: I personally pressed up one thousand copies of a 7" EP· featuring "Another One Rides the Bus" and drove around to various Los Angeles record stores, allowing them to sell it "on consignment."

★ Those crazy patchwork-quilt velvet pants—a gift from a friend in college—
were worn in every single live show for those first few years.

Westwood One engendered some surreal moments, like when Al would make calls on Westwood One's behalf and the person on the other end of the line would ask if they were talking to *the* Al Yankovic of "Another One Rides the Bus" and "My Bologna" fame.

With a diploma in hand and a day job to help pay the rent, Yankovic earnestly set about making a go of it in the music industry. When Yankovic had trouble interesting major labels in his silly songs, he borrowed money from his mentor, Dr. Demento, and pressed one thousand homemade copies of the *Another One Rides the Bus* EP on Placebo Records in 1981.

Al had a vision. He had a drummer. He was driven. He needed someone to take him to the next step professionally. He needed a guiding hand to help him navigate the tricky waters of the music business. Enter Jay Levey. Levey's professional path began after discovering a beat-up paperback copy of Timothy Leary's *Confessions of a Hope Fiend* while bumming around the country post-college. Levey

★ Ah, the marquis for the infamous Missing Persons concert at the Santa Monica Civic. Whenever someone comes up to me and says, "Hey! I saw you at that show!" I say, "Really? What did *you* throw at me?"

was instantly riveted by the charismatic countercultural icon and set about meeting him despite Leary's incarceration. After Leary's release from prison, Levey became his friend, roommate, and assistant, helping Leary with his speaking engagements, but eventually Levey's muse cried out for something more creative.

Levey wanted to help shape and steer careers. He began with Dr. Demento. Levey helped Demento put together a live DJ and film show for colleges and clubs, and Demento invited star attraction Al to perform. In a Pheonix, Arizona, nightclub some time in 1981, Levey watched as the hungry young performer barreled through a twenty-minute set with just his accordion, and was blown away by his charisma. Levey knew talent when he saw it, and the kid with the accordion possessed that ineffable quality known as star power.

Things began happening for Al. Radio had not yet become the rigidly formatted straitjacket it is today, so Al could walk into the studio of KROQ in Los Angles and hand DJ Jed the Fish a copy of his new single and Jed would turn around and

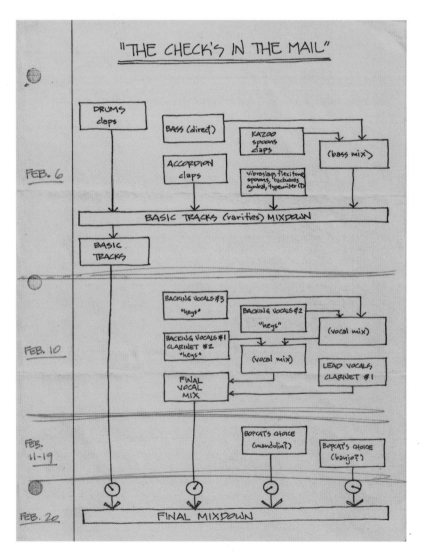

★ In the early '80s, all of my recordings for Dr. Demento were done on a 4-track TEAC cassette portastudio. Since everything eventually had to wind up on four tracks, I would have to plan out my recording sequence, as shown in this chart.

★ In the studio with Mr. Rock and Roll Hoochie Koo himself,
Rick Derringer—the producer of my first six albums.

★ When I walked onto the set of the "Ricky" video dressed as Ricky Ricardo, some of my closest friends didn't even recognize me. We were extremely fortunate to hire soon-to-be-world-famous voiceover artist Tress MacNeille, who knocked it out of the park as Lucy.

play the song on the air immediately. Which is what he did. Al was getting play on *The Dr. Demento Show* and KROQ. Al had a drummer (Schwartz) and a manager (Levey). Now he needed a band. He held auditions and hired Steve Jay as his bassist and Steve's friend Jim West as his guitarist. Along with Jon "Bermuda" Schwartz, they remain with Al to this day. In 1991 Rubén Valtierra joined the band on keyboards to fill out the sound.

So the weird kid with the accordion had a band, a manager, a single on a major label, and his very own underground EP. If Yankovic's boyhood dream of becoming a writer and cartoonist for *MAD* had struck his guidance counselor as prohibitively difficult, the notion that Yankovic would make a living as a troubador who traveled the country changing the lyrics to popular songs so that they're about junk food and TV would have struck the guidance counselor as insane. Weird. Mad, even.

Weird Al was growing in confidence with each performance, except for an ill-fated gig where Yankovic opened for New Wave hit-makers Missing Persons and was pelted with projectiles by enraged Missing Persons fans. Not everyone, it seems, was ready for the ascent of "Weird Al" Yankovic. Yankovic's lingering memory of the night is of Jon frantically picking up the loose change they had been pelted with. In those lean early years, every nickel counted.

Al had scored a single on a major label and serious airplay. In 1982 he set his sights on landing a contract for an entire album. He needed a producer. In another fortuitous coincidence, when Jay Levey asked manager/songwriter Jake Hooker for permission for Al to parody his song "I Love Rock 'n' Roll" (originally recorded by

★ The cover for the "Ricky" single was illustrated by Rogerio, the same artist who did my first album cover.

Hooker's band the Arrows and popularized by Joan Jett and the Blackhearts) as "I Love Rocky Road," Hooker instantly agreed. He also mentioned that one of his clients, virtuoso guitarist and "Rock and Roll, Hoochie Coo" hit-maker Rick Derringer, just happened to be an established producer of hits (for acts like Edgar Winter Group) and was looking for clients.

It was kismet. Scoring a hotshot guitar hero with a past that included opening gigs for Led Zeppelin *and* the Rolling Stones as the producer for a debut album by a rela-

TWEET

Whenever I hear somebody use the word "literally" incorrectly, it literally makes my brain explode.

NOTES TO HOLLYWOOD

I think the movie *Bewitched* would've been a lot better if Jim Carrey replaced Will Ferrell halfway through and nobody said a word about it.

The Special Edition DVD of *The King's Speech* should have a blooper reel—it'd just be a bunch of takes of Colin Firth enunciating his lines perfectly.

I think Hollywood should do yet another reboot of *Footloose*, except this time focusing more on the horrible effects of leprosy.

Great Movie Idea: Two people meet. They hate each other at first, but then . . . they wind up falling in love! (You're welcome, Hollywood.)

Hey, you know what else would be a really cool subject matter for a movie and/or TV show? Vampires.

★ Besides the inhumanly long hours and the tiny budget, the worst part of the "I Love Rocky Road" video shoot was having to eat the ice cream—it was really just painted mashed potatoes (so nothing would melt under the hot lights).

★ This cover doesn't work as well on a CD—but it came out in the days
of the 12" LP, when you could appreciate the details in album art. Every
song on the album is visually referenced somewhere on this cover.

tively unknown artist was a major coup. Meanwhile, Jake also had a friend who owned Cherokee Studios in Hollywood and was willing to let Al record an album there on spec. The studio was willing to take a chance on the young musician but not *too* much of a chance.

The recording of Al's self-titled 1983 debut was fast, cheap, and loose. There was no time to refine and perfect and polish songs to a blinding sheen. Al, his band, and his new producer only had enough time to bang out passable versions of songs from Al's ever-growing catalog and hope for the best. Sometimes Al didn't even have time for that; the version of "Another One Rides the Bus" found on the LP is the same version Dr. Demento recorded back in 1980.

The abundant rough edges on *"Weird Al" Yankovic* provide much of its ramshackle charm. "Happy Birthday" introduces a recurring theme in Al's oeuvre: holidays as trials of the damned. Let other singers serenade happy little birthday boys and girls on their special day; only Yankovic uses a birthday song to remind listeners that "a million people every day are starvin' in the street" while "your daddy's in the gutter with the wretched and the poor." It is Al's oddball homage to New Wave cult star Tonio K., and it gets bleaker and bleaker until Al is all but welcoming the probability of a nuclear holocaust.

"Happy Birthday" epitomizes a pervasive streak of morbidity in Al's music that would find its purest expression in both its focus on the ever-looming threat of a nuclear war and its evisceratingly dark take on holidays. On 1986's *Polka Party!*, "Christmas at Ground Zero" would fuse these threads together to create arguably the most depressing Christmas song ever.

The *"Weird Al" Yankovic* album cover doubles as a statement of purpose. Al was an unabashed pop-culture obsessive before it was cool. He was a geek before it was cool. He was uncool before being uncool became cool. "Weird Al" Yankovic didn't just wear his influences proudly; he paid reverent homage to them on the album cover. Al chose Brazilian artist Rogerio to do the cover artwork because his detailed style hearkened back to Al's beloved *MAD* magazine. On the cover, Al dreams of mak-

GRAMMATICALLY CORRECT SONGS

You're the One Whom I Want
(John Travolta and Olivia Newton-John)

Tie My Kangaroo Down, Sport
(Rolf Harris)

I Can't Get Any Satisfaction
(Rolling Stones)

Whip It Well *(Devo)*

Lie Lady Lie *(Bob Dylan)*

ing the impossible leap from accordion-stroking geek to rock god while surrounded by pop-culture detritus as well as tributes to seminal influences like Allan Sherman and Dr. Demento.

Considering Al's genius for inhabiting the divergent personas of eccentric pop stars while retaining his own identity, it's fitting that he begins his first album by assuming the rich Cuban accent of Ricky Ricardo for "Ricky," a loving tribute to Lucille Ball and *I Love Lucy* and a parody of Toni Basil's hit "Mickey."

To find the perfect Lucy to his Ricky, Al put out an ad in a local paper seeking the services of a Lucille Ball impersonator. He received two responses. Fortunately, one was from Tress MacNeille, a struggling actress and voiceover artist with a bad cold that made her sound even more like Ball. MacNeille was the perfect Lucy to Al's characteristi-

cifically to see Yankovic. The ecstatic audience response to Yankovic's ever-increasing string of hits betrayed the happy accident that the featured attraction had become the headliner. Soon the billing for gigs reflected it.

No one could have been prouder of Al's success than Demento, with the possible exception of Al's parents, who doted on their only child and took great pride in his achievements.

"Weird Al" Yankovic had a number of factors working against it commercially. Scotti Brothers, the label Yankovic eventually signed with under its Rock 'n Roll Records imprint after striking out with other labels, was not exactly a commercial powerhouse, although it'd had some success in the 1970s with bubblegum pop star Leif Garrett. "Another One Rides the Bus" was almost three years old and a fan favorite on *The Dr. Demento Show* when

TWEET | I ask nicely, you ask nicely, we ALL ask nicely for ice cream! #takeitdownanotch

cally suave Ricky. She even looked the part, which came in handy when it came time to shoot the video.

"Ricky" is less a spoof of *I Love Lucy* than a valentine. Al's affection for the show is evident even before "Ricky" segues smoothly into a snazzy variation of the *I Love Lucy* theme. Al wrote about junk food and TV and pop culture because it spoke to him. If Al enjoyed a love-hate relationship with pop culture, it was freighted heavily toward the "love" side of the equation. Pop culture returned Al's affection. In his archives, Al has a lovely thank-you letter Lucille Ball sent him in appreciation.

Weird Al was the featured attraction of Dr. Demento's live shows at college campuses and the like but in 1984 Al's popularity eclipsed that of his mentor, and Al and his band became the headliners while Dr. Demento became the supporting act. Audiences increasingly came to shows spe-

"Weird Al" Yankovic was released. And MacNeille wasn't able to tour, so that fact limited the commercial potential of the song "Ricky."

So while *"Weird Al" Yankovic* was a modest success and would eventually go gold, it was far from a monster hit.

CHAPTER 2

The EAT IT GUY

JUST 500 POUNDS

BEFORE

AFTER

SLIMMER TRIMMER

TERRIFIED HOUSEWIFE EATS HER OWN FOOT

EXCLUSIVE PHOTOS INSIDE! PAGE 12

MIDNIGHT Star JULY 25, 1984 50¢

New Scientific Report:
**Doctors Reveal—
Broccoli Makes
You Smarter**

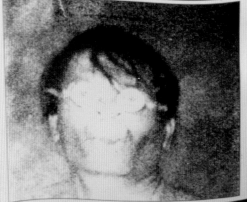

**LIZ AND DICK—
ARE THEY REALLY
ANCIENT
ASTRONAUTS?**

THE INCREDIBLE
FROG BOY—
WHAT DOES HE
WANT FROM US?

PLAY JINGO!

THE REAL UNTOLD
STORY BEHIND
LONI ANDERSON'S
HUSH-HUSH HEAD
TRANSPLANT

**NOW IT CAN BE TOLD:
MICHAEL JACKSON WON'T GIVE US AN INTERVIEW**

★ Inquiring minds want to know!

AL NEEDED SOMETHING EXTRA TO BREAK THROUGH. HE NEEDED A NEW MEDIUM IN WHICH HE WOULDN'T JUST SING OR PLAY ACCORDION; HE WOULD ENTERTAIN. HE NEEDED A MEDIUM THAT WOULD ALLOW HIM TO TRY OUT OUTRAGEOUS COSTUMES AND INSANE CHARACTERS.

Al needed, in other words, a medium that didn't really exist in 1979, when he released "My Bologna," but that would eventually play a defining role in his career: the music video. In 1983, MTV was a hungry young cable network with not much in the way of money and vast oceans of time to fill, and Weird Al was an equally hungry young musician with boundless enthusiasm, all the energy and focus in the world, and a gift for visual humor. Weird Al and a network that promised to play nothing but a weird new medium called the music video were a perfect fit. When it came to making music videos, Al was, as always, an eager student and a quick study. He took to the filmmaking process naturally and played a big

★ I always enjoy rubbing elbows with my peers in the comedy community.

role alongside manager and music video director Levey in determining the look and feel of his iconic 1980s videos.

MTV had made Al a star. Al made the network safe for comedy. MTV was so enamored of its resident jester that on April Fool's Day 1984, it gave Al four hours to program and host the very first installment of *AL-TV*. It's impossible to imagine the network giving over such a massive chunk of programming to even the biggest pop star these days, but back in the early days MTV was desperate for programming and crazy about Al.

Al was responsible for the segments that ran between music videos. The most crowd-pleasing and memorable element of *AL-TV* consisted of "celebrity

interviews" that took preexisting footage of big pop stars jibber-jabbering and edited it together with new footage of Al asking new questions designed to make the subject of the interview look as ridiculous as possible. When the pop star in question was Boy George, the unwitting first celebrity to "talk" to Al for *AL-TV,* that wasn't difficult.

Al's hilarious fake celebrity interviews found him doing on television what he'd been doing musically: riffing gleefully on the absurdity of pop stars and conducting a very funny, very one-sided conversation with pop music.

On MTV and everywhere else there was no bigger star than Michael Jackson. He defined the medium. It became synonymous with him. Jackson's incredible popularity did not escape Al. In concerts, Al would perform a medley of food-themed ditties. The medley always went over well but a snippet of a "Beat It" parody called "Eat It" got an especially ecstatic reaction, so he fleshed it out into a full song.

The whimsical former Jackson 5 frontman happily agreed to the parody and "Eat It" was born. Yankovic was already tiring of being known as the parody guy, so he asked his record label if it might consider releasing a terrific original composition called "Midnight Star" as the first single from his second album, which would be called *"Weird Al" Yankovic in 3-D*, but cooler heads prevailed.

"Eat It" exploded. If "My Bologna," "Another One Rides the Bus," "I Love Rocky Road," and *"Weird Al" Yankovic* got Al's foot in the door, "Eat It" kicked it down. Yankovic was an overnight sensation nearly a decade in the making. The genius of the "Eat It" video lies in its simplicity. In keeping with Al's desire for parodies to resemble the originals as closely as possible, the video for "Eat It" is essentially a shot-by-shot remake of "Beat It," only funny and with a shockingly young and skinny rapacious Al as a bizarro-world Michael Jackson, filled with

★ This is the makeshift, no-budget set of *AL-TV,* where MTV basically gave me hours of programming time to do *anything I wanted*.

★ One time I did the weather for a news show in Cleveland. I think I announced that the earth was going to crash into the sun and we were all gonna die. For some reason, they never invited me back.

 TWEET | AHHH! OH GOD I'M DYING! NOOO!!! I—
Oh, wait, I had a beet salad last night.

a Jewish mother's angry insistence that you enjoy a nice nosh rather than Jackson's vague anti-gang rhetoric.

One of the many places "Eat It" hit was Japan. The country provided the setting for what is easily the most surreal moment of Al's career, if not the history of the universe. Yankovic was invited to appear on what he was told was Japan's *Saturday Night Live,* despite the

★ In the early days when we were touring with Dr. Demento, the band didn't travel in a bus. We took turns driving across the country in a motorhome, often in the freezing cold. Actually, I never had to drive—at the time I was too young to be covered by the insurance policy! (L to R: Bermuda, Dr. Demento, me, Jim West, and Steve Jay)

minor handicap of not speaking Japanese. Sporting a look of panic mixed with desperation and soul-shaking terror, Al stumbled his way dazed through a strange scenario involving women dressed as Geishas, a man heralded as the Japanese John Belushi either doing a frantic dance or suffering an epileptic seizure, and, climactically, Al performing a mostly English, partially

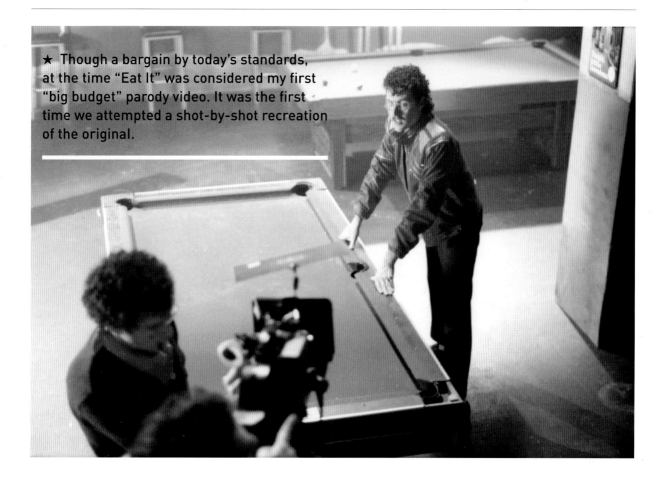

★ Though a bargain by today's standards, at the time "Eat It" was considered my first "big budget" parody video. It was the first time we attempted a shot-by-shot recreation of the original.

phonetic Japanese version of "Eat It" while Sumo wrestlers dance and a man dressed like a morbidly obese Asian Michael Jackson gorges himself on noodles.

Then things got a little strange. A man dressed as a giant lobster was brought onstage and Al attempted to eat him. Through it all Al wears a look of existential terror that deepens by the moment.

Nevertheless, Japan embraced this odd American who sang about food and TV shows and danced like Michael Jackson and played the accordion. "Eat It" was released in Japan with a sleeve depicting a Weird Al/Michael Jackson hybrid. Speaking of hybrids, Al's first official album release in Japan was a combination of tracks from *"Weird Al" Yankovic* and *"Weird Al" Yankovic in 3-D*, along

TWEET | 1. Kill Hitler 2. Buy Apple stock 3. Turn off that downstairs faucet #TimeMachineChecklist

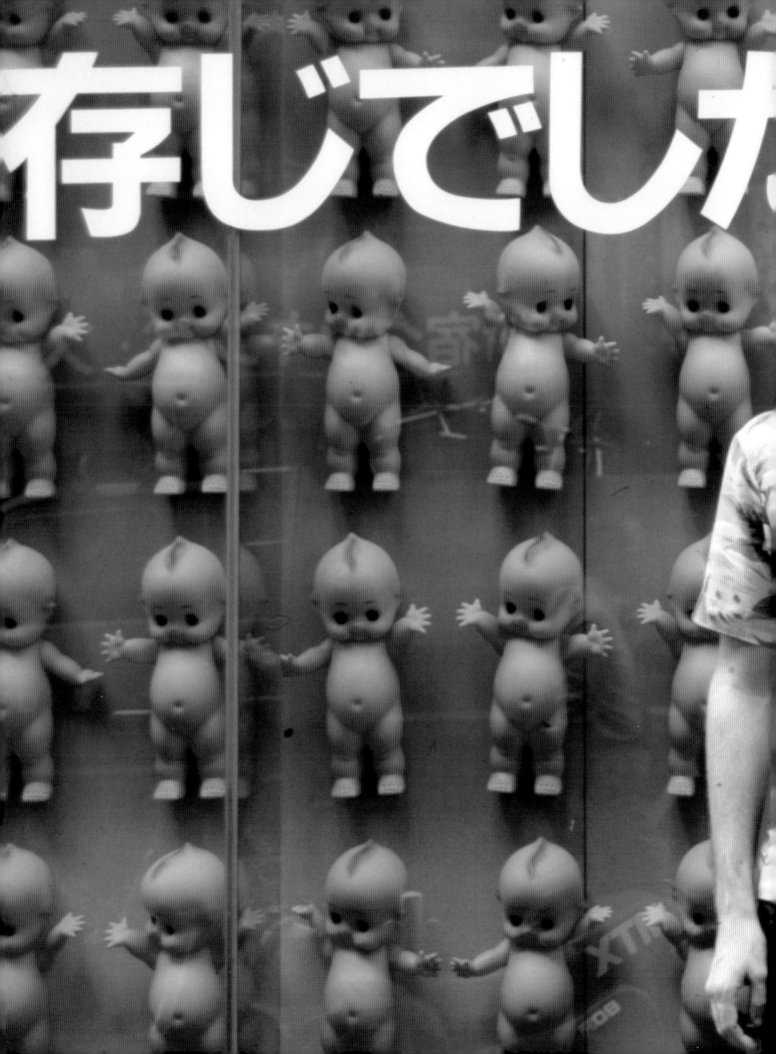

こか？キュ

★ This is what I look like standing in front of a wall of babies in Japan.

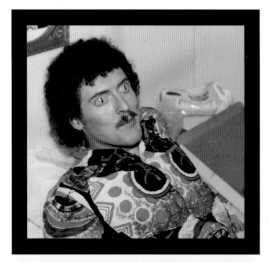

with a non-vocal version of "Eat It" ostensibly identical to "Beat It." Al found Japan's early love for him both flattering and mildly bewildering.

Seemingly overnight, Weird Al became the "Eat It" guy. All those rocky-road-ice-cream-eating contests and coffeehouse gigs and playing for fraternity parties he'd endured along the way had paid off. And "Eat It" wasn't just nominated for a 1984 Grammy; it won. Al could say good-bye to his day job. The mailroom would have to get along without him. Weird Al had found his calling as the world's least likely rock star. He didn't drink. He didn't use drugs. He left hotel rooms shamefully un-trashed, and he wasn't about to blow the money that started rolling in on solid gold Humvees or diamond-studded swimming pools.

★ I discovered that it was extremely challenging to attempt comedy in a country where English is not the primary language. Subtle wordplay simply did not translate well—I found myself resorting to very broad slapstick. Soon I was performing with dancing Sumo wrestlers and guys in lobster suits.

In 3-D wasn't just Al's first bona fide hit album and the LP that gave the world "Eat It." It was also a huge step up creatively. A bigger budget and more time in the studio had given Al, returning producer Rick Derringer, and Al's band the opportunity to smooth away some of the rough edges of the debut and deliver a much more polished album.

In 3-D might just be Al's masterpiece. The Bob Marley–style reggae number "Buy Me a Condo" satirizes the manic materialism of the Reagan '80s through the first-person narrative of a rugged islander who traded in hanging with the rude boys and ragamuffins for Izod shirts and Jackson Browne CDs. On "I Lost on Jeopardy," his parody of the Greg Kihn Band's hit "Jeopardy," Al winks back at the life that might have been when he sings warily of competing on the show against "a plumber and an architect, both with a PhD."

7Y0059 STEREO ¥700

"Weird Al" Yankovic
Eat It

事情通にバカ受け！ 歯ごたえ十分の、
人を喰ったデビュー・シングル。
マイケル・ジャクソン(作詞・作曲)今夜は
ビート・イット』のパロディ、遂に登場!!

プロデュース
＆
ギター・ソロ

リック・デリンジャー

今夜も EAT IT

ロスの笑売人タル・ヤンコビック

"Weird Al" Yankovic

●SIDE・B あいつのロック・ン・ロール・ランチ

Produced by Rick Derringer for High Calibre Productions.

★ When I visited Japan in 1984, I discovered that—surprise!—all of my singles and albums over there had completely different (and usually much better) cover art.

★ "Eat It" by Alex Pardee

★ This is the most starstruck I've ever been in my life. I tried to have a normal, pleasant conversation with him, but the whole time my brain was screaming, *"You're talking to Paul McCartney!"*

★ This is me channeling Sting for the "King of Suede" single cover photo shoot. Oddly enough, that is *not* a wig—they straightened and frosted my actual hair.

★ Sometimes, in order to get from one place to another, the band would have to board a heavier-than-air flying machine.

  TWEET "It's hard to pick a candidate to vote for— they're just all so wonderful!" —I'm guessing no one, in any election, ever

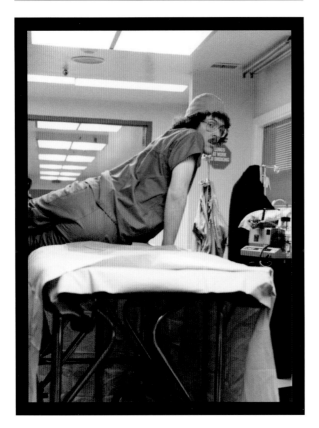

★ Writhing around on hospital gurneys had always been a hobby of mine, so it just felt very natural to do it in a music video.

The drive-in movie homage "Nature Trail to Hell," B-52s pastiche "Mr. Popeil," "Midnight Star" (an Al original), the Survivor parody "Theme from Rocky XIII" (aka The Rye or the Kaiser), and a spoof of Men Without Hats' "The Safety Dance" called "The Brady Bunch" all delight in the trashiest recesses of pop culture, in infomercials and cynical sequels and campy horror movies. They're celebrations of American vulgarity, tongue-in-cheek odes to the white noise that makes up much of contemporary pop culture.

Al's powers were growing. Merv Griffin claims the popularity of 1984's "I Lost on Jeopardy" inspired him to re-launch the show, this time with a deliciously condescending Canadian named Alex Trebek as host.

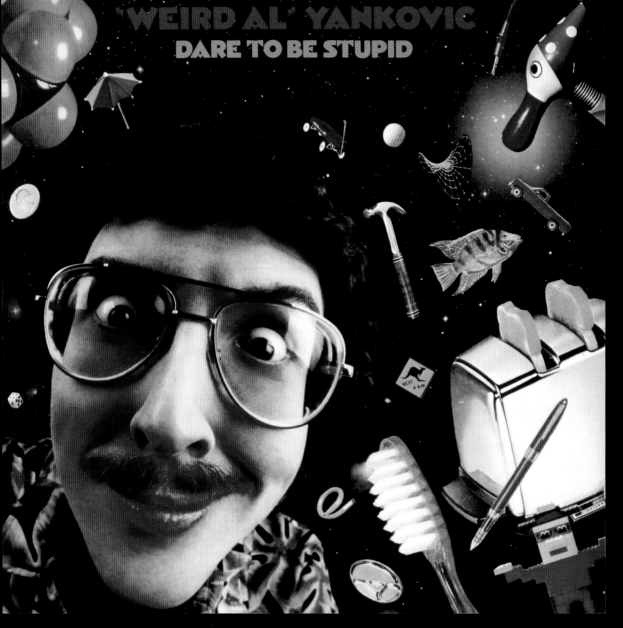

'WEIRD AL' YANKOVIC
DARE TO BE STUPID

★ I remember the art department at CBS was impressed by my apparent lack of vanity—apparently none of their other artists ever wanted a distorted fish-eye picture of themselves on a record cover.

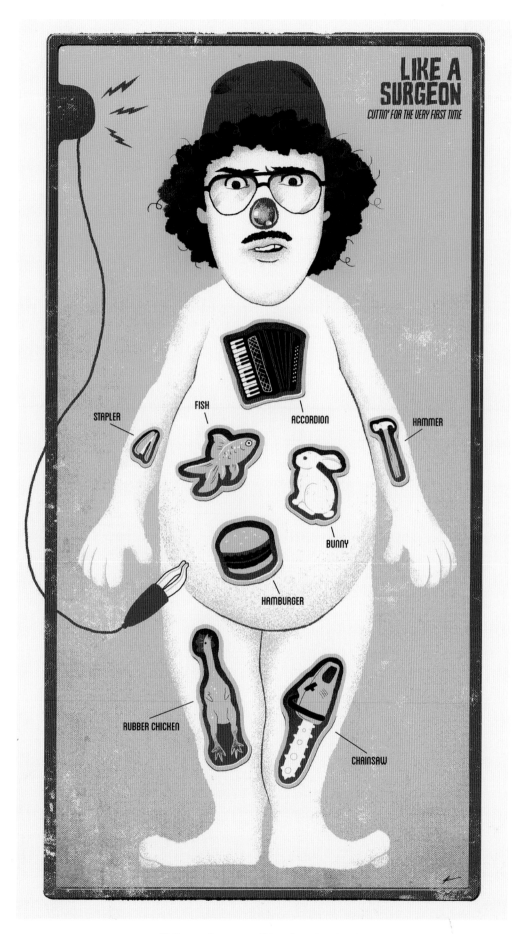

★ "Like a Surgeon" by Justin Erickson

TWEET

Haven't heard anything lately, but I hope by now they've determined who exactly let the dogs out and that they've been punished accordingly.

The inspiration for Al's next music video smash, and a track that would appear on his third studio album, came from either the likeliest or unlikeliest possible place. According to Weird Al lore, Madonna was walking down the street one day when she told her friend that Weird Al should parody "Like a Virgin" as "Like a Surgeon." The friend just so happened to be a friend of Jay Levey, who in turn relayed the news/suggestion to Al. Al happily acquiesced; though he only learned of Madonna's suggestion secondhand, he wants her to know that she should feel free to pitch ideas to him whenever she sees fit.

With each new single, Al's stage show grew. Now Al had an ever-growing catalog of hits to dip into, each with a ubiquitous video generally riffing on *another* ubiquitous video. The sight of Al putting on the "Eat It" jacket inspired Pavlovian chills of anticipation from diehard fans who knew

★ One of the many images from the "Dare to Be Stupid" music video that are much too profound and complex for mere mortals to comprehend.

★ Another snazzy ensemble from the "Dare to Be Stupid" video shoot.

I've got this horrible feeling that the VHS tape rewinder I bought in the '80s is starting to lose some of its resale value.

TWEET

what that outfit change inevitably signaled. Video had been a core part of the Al stage show since he would show the "Ricky" music video during appearances with Dr. Demento, but Al's show was rapidly turning into a full-on multimedia extravaganza filled with videos, extensive costume changes, and increasingly elaborate choreography. Al wasn't just a singer anymore; he was a consummate entertainer.

And backing Weird Al required a formidable set of skills as well. West, Schwartz, Jay, and Valtierra didn't just have to be more than proficient in just about every genre of music, from polka to country to hard rock to hip-hop; they also had to be performers adept at keeping

★ On the Prohibition-era nightclub set for the "This Is the Life" music video, Jim West stood out as the anachronistic heavy metal guitar soloist.

the show moving and the songs tight during an insanely complicated live spectacle involving constant costume changes, bits, banter, video, and choreography. The road warriors in Al's band consequently aren't just terrific, versatile musicians; they're also dynamite entertainers who have remained a tight, cohesive, and consistent unit for going on three decades.

Television loved Al, so it only made sense that soon the big screen would follow suit. The people behind the Michael Keaton mob comedy *Johnny Dangerously* hired Al to make a theme song and music video for the film's soundtrack. The track "This Is the Life"

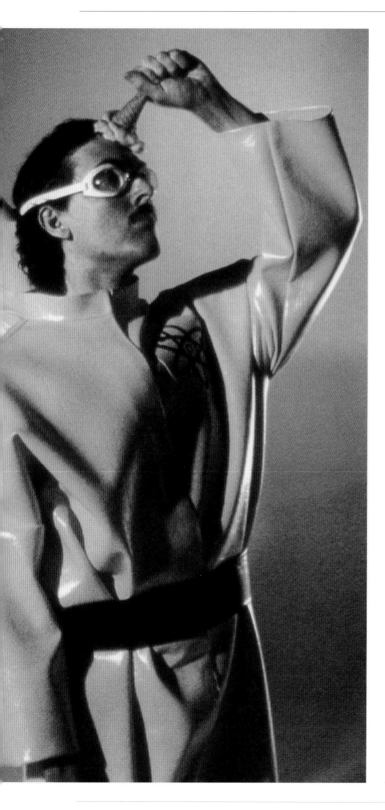

ended up appearing on Al's 1985 album *Dare to Be Stupid*. The album as a whole betrayed Al's profound interest in the big screen. The title track, a loving homage to Devo, would be chosen for the soundtrack on the 1986 animated *Transformers* movie, "Slime Creatures from Outer Space" paid homage to 1950s sci-fi movies, and "Yoda" marked Al's maiden exploration of the cinematic universe of *Star Wars*.

Al had movies on the mind. He was rapidly branching off into new fields. In August 1985, Al, Jay Levey, and film producer Robert K. Weiss (*The Naked Gun*) made a tongue-in-cheek "biographical" long-form video called

★ Back when the music industry was doing a little better, we had the budget to rent as many plastic cows as we wanted!

The Compleat Al, along with a literary companion piece that quickly raced out of print entitled *The Authorized Al.* They were both fundamentally silly larks, offhanded goofs. Al and Jay were much more serious about the film they were writing for Al to star in. Ah, but that is a story—and a heartbreak—for later.

Yankovic's continuing success and unexpected longevity delighted his bosses over at Scotti Brothers. He was the label's only consistent hit-maker, so he felt a lot

DARE TO BE STUPID

by AL YANKOVIC

Put down that chain saw and listen to me
It's time for us to join in the fight
It's time to let your babies grow up to be cowboys
It's time to let the bedbugs bite
You better put all your eggs in one basket
You better count your chickens before they hatch
You better sell some wine before its time
You better find yourself an itch to scratch

You better squeeze all the Charmin you can
When Mr. Whipple's not around
Stick your head in the microwave
and get yourself a tan

Talk with your mouth full
Bite the hand that feeds you
Bite off more then you can chew
What can you do?
Dare to be stupid
Take some wooden nickels
Look for Mr. Goodbar
Get your mojo working now
I'll show you how
You can dare to be stupid

You can turn the other cheek
You can just give up the ship
You can eat a bunch of sushi then forget to leave a tip
Dare to be stupid
Come on and dare to be stupid
It's so easy to do
We're all waiting for you
Let's go!

It's time to make a mountain out of a molehill
So can I have a volunteer?
There's no more time for crying over spilled milk
Now it's time for crying in your beer
Settle down, raise a family, join the PTA
Buy some sensible shoes and a Chevrolet
Then ***party till you're broke*** and they drag you away
It's okay
You can dare to be stupid

It's like spitting on a fish
It's like barking up a tree
It's like I said, you gotta buy one if you wanna get one free
Dare to be stupid
Yes . . . why don't you dare to be stupid?
It's so easy, so easy to do
We're all waiting for you

Burn your candle at both ends
Look a gift horse in the mouth
Mashed potatoes can be your friends

You can be a coffee achiever
You can sit around the house and watch *Leave It to Beaver*
The future's up to you, so what you gonna do?
Dare to be stupid! Dare to be stupid!

What did I say?
Tell me what did I say?
It's all right
We can be stupid all night
Come on, join the crowd
Shout it out loud
I can't hear you
Okay, I can hear you now
Let's go!
Dare to be stupid (repeat 3x)

★ "Dare to Be Stupid" by Graham Erwin

★ A production still from *The Compleat Al*. Really, what family *wouldn't* want a set of Weird Al lookalike kits?

★ As is the case with most professional singer-songwriters, occasionally my band has to break me out of a creative funk by dunking my head in a huge tub of yogurt.

of pressure from the label to keep cranking out product. When Al didn't deliver an album of new material quickly enough, the label resorted to endlessly repackaging its marquee artist's back catalog. A mere five years into his career as a Scotti Brothers artist, the label released Al's first greatest hits album in 1988. A second album of greatest hits followed six years later, as did a full-on box set (*Permanent Record: Al in the Box*).

Al's fans had always been unusually devoted to him, and he reciprocated that devotion. Even after physically exhausting live performances he'd stick around after shows to sign autographs and interact with fans during meet-and-greets. So the idea of making fans pay for songs they'd already purchased in a different context distressed Al.

Al registered an exquisitely passive-aggressive protest against Scotti Brothers' eagerness to bleed his catalog dry via the artwork on 1994's *The Food Album*: the cover of the food-themed compilation depicts a grotesque monster crudely flossing its teeth after having literally picked the desiccated corpse of Weird Al clean. If Scotti Brothers comprehended Al's bleak joke, it didn't keep them from releasing the album with the cover all the same.

Scotti Brothers was always looking for ways to maximize a musical roster that combined established talents like Al with newcomers and journeymen. In the mid-1980s, the label scored a minor victory when it signed James Brown and scored a modest hit in "Living in America"—Brown's big number from the *Rocky IV* soundtrack.

So in 1986 when it came time for Al to pick a song to parody for the first single off his fourth album, which would bear the unfortunate title *Polka Party!* (an album title only slightly more commercial than *Please Don't Buy This Al-*

★ Not many people remember that I was one of the original members of Run DMC. Unfortunately we had to part ways due to creative/fashion differences.

bum), Scotti Brothers had some very strong ideas about what Al should spoof, and that unsurprisingly involved keeping it all in the Scotti Brothers family. So "Living in America" became the funny but ill-fated "Living with a Hernia."

With the benefit of hindsight, it's now apparent that painful medical procedures are not the most commercial subject for funny songs. Not even Al's crowd-pleasing recitation of the various different kinds of hernias one can contract—incomplete, epigastric, bladder, strangulated, lumbar, Richter's, obstructed, inguinal, and direct—was enough to keep the song from dying a quick death on the charts.

 TWEET | Hey Mr. Tambourine Man, guess what? All of your songs pretty much sound the same. You play a stinking TAMBOURINE.

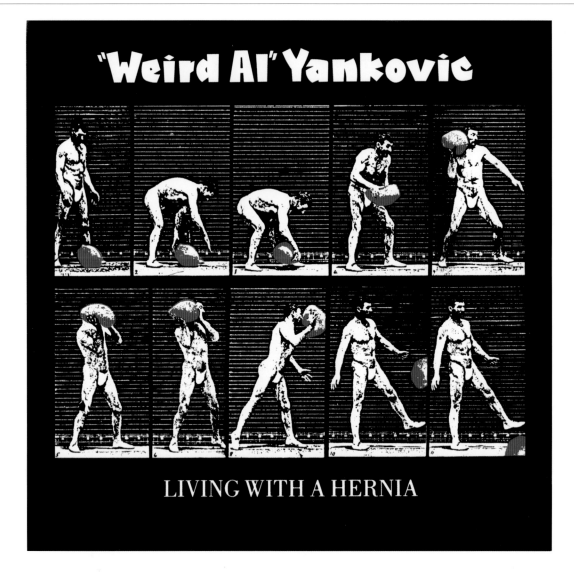

A strong, mainstream commercial sensibility had long coexisted within Al's psyche alongside a demented prankster's streak that delights in upending expectations. The demented prankster seemed to have taken over during *Polka Party!* The problems began with its title, seemingly designed to scare away fans attracted by the promise of the next "Eat It." By that point, Al was a huge pop star. So why did his new album title make it seem as though he was inexplicably trying to win over polka partisans at the expense of his devoted mainstream audience? The album's cover, meanwhile, further divided the album's potential audience by showing a gleeful, accordion-toting Al surrounded by a motley aggregation of New Wave freaks. If Al had deliberately set out to sabotage his album's commercial chances, he couldn't have done a better job.

★ The cover of the "Living with a Hernia" single had to done in a hurry, so the art department just slapped on the first hernia-related clip art they could find. *Voila!*

★ I had my skeleton removed at an early age just so
I could do stupid stuff like this whenever I felt like it.

★ The band and I desperately try to find our inspiration in the recording studio in this still from *The Compleat Al*.

TWEET

If you carbon-coat every specimen to increase its scanning signal . . . YOU MIGHT BE AN ELECTRON MICROSCOPIST. #FailedJeffFoxworthyRoutines

YANKOVIC
BEACON THEATRE—OCT. 5

Dare to be Stupid

Photo by: Peter Cunningham

**"DARE TO BE STUPID" THE NEW ALBUM FROM "WEIRD AL" YANKOVIC
ON SCOTTI BROS/CBS RECORDS & TAPES**

Beacon Theatre Ticket info: $16.50 & $14.50 on sale now at the
Beacon Box Office (787-1477) and all Ticketron outlets (977-9020).
To Charge Tickets—call Chargit (944-9300) or Teletron (947-5850)

COME MEET WEIRD AL • SAT OCTOBER 5TH AT VIDEO SHACK (Broadway and 49th Street) 1-3PM

★ This poster for my show at New York's Beacon Theatre was a direct rip-off of (ahem, I mean *homage to*) Springsteen's iconic poster for his shows at the Bottom Line.

ONE MORE
MINUTE

by AL YANKOVIC

Well, I heard that you're leavin'

Gonna leave me far behind

'Cause you found a brand-new lover

You decided that I'm not your kind

So I pulled your name out of my Rolodex

And I tore all your pictures in two

And ***I burned down the malt shop
        where we used to go***

Just because it reminds me of you

That's right, you ain't gonna see me cryin'

I'm glad that you found somebody new

'Cause I'd rather spend eternity eating shards of broken glass

Than spend one more minute with you

I guess I might seem kinda bitter

You got me feelin' down in the dumps

'Cause ***I'm stranded all alone in
        the gas station of love***

And I have to use the self-service pumps

Oh, so honey, let me help you with that suitcase

You ain't gonna break my heart in two

'Cause I'd rather get a hundred thousand paper cuts on my face

Than spend one more minute with you

I'd rather rip out my intestines with a fork

Than watch you going out with other men

I'd rather slam my fingers in a door

Again and again and again and again and again

Aw, can't you see what I'm tryin' to say, darlin'?

I'd rather have my blood sucked out by leeches

Shove an ice pick under a toenail or two

I'd rather clean all the bathrooms in Grand Central Station
        with my tongue

Than spend one more minute with you

Yes, I'd rather jump naked on a huge pile of thumbtacks

Or stick my nostrils together with Krazy Glue

***I'd rather dive into a swimming pool
        filled with double-edged razor blades***

Than spend one more minute with you

I'd rather rip my heart right out of my rib cage with my bare
        hands

And then throw it on the floor and stomp on it till I die

Than spend one more minute . . .

With you

★ On the set of the "One More Minute" video. I believe we were attempting to pose like an early Beatles publicity shot.

TWEET

Al Pacino rarely discusses his unfortunately named twin brothers Cap and Frap.

TWEET

Our family hiking motto:
Take Only Memories, Leave Only Corpses

★ We shot the video for "Living with a Hernia" with real showgirls on the same stage in Las Vegas (Bally's) where James Brown had originally performed "Living in America" for *Rocky IV*.

★ In retrospect, this was probably not my most mass-appeal album cover.
It was only popular with hard-core punks and polka enthusiasts.

As a final defiant gesture to commercial considerations, Al finally gave in and gave his record label the Christmas song they'd wanted for years. In keeping with Al's penchant for gallows humor and subverting expectations, Al delivered the grimmest Yuletide tune imaginable: a nuclear-apocalypse-themed ditty called "Christmas at Ground Zero" that eagerly anticipated atomic annihilation. When the label refused to pay for a music video—it inexplicably doubted the commercial potential of a nuclear-holocaust-themed Christmas song that didn't reference a single form of hernia—Al went ahead and made his directorial debut with a video assembled largely from Cold War–era footage in the public domain.

Polka Party! halted Yankovic's winning streak. It peaked at number 177 despite containing one of Al's strongest and most personal songs, the Talking Heads homage "Dog Eat Dog." As with the title song from *Dare to Be Stupid,* Al's affection for the New Wave weirdos he

★ In 1987 I was the opening act for The Monkees (something *else* I have in common with Jimi Hendrix)! At the Greek Theatre, the guys thought it would be fun for me to come on stage dressed as Michael Nesmith (who had declined to tour with them). It turned out to be one of those "better on paper" ideas.

FAMOUS QUOTES

"You can fool some of the people all of the time, and . . . okay, let's just go with that one."
—*Rupert Murdoch*

"Mortality! ACK!!"
—*Cathy, on her death bed*

"Pose! Pose again! Do another pose!"
—*Inarticulate Fashion Photographer*

"Oy, You're KILLING Me with This Song . . . and So Softly!"
—*Jewish Roberta Flack*

"Well, I'M certainly not Spartacus!"
—*Some guy in the crowd who clearly doesn't understand memes*

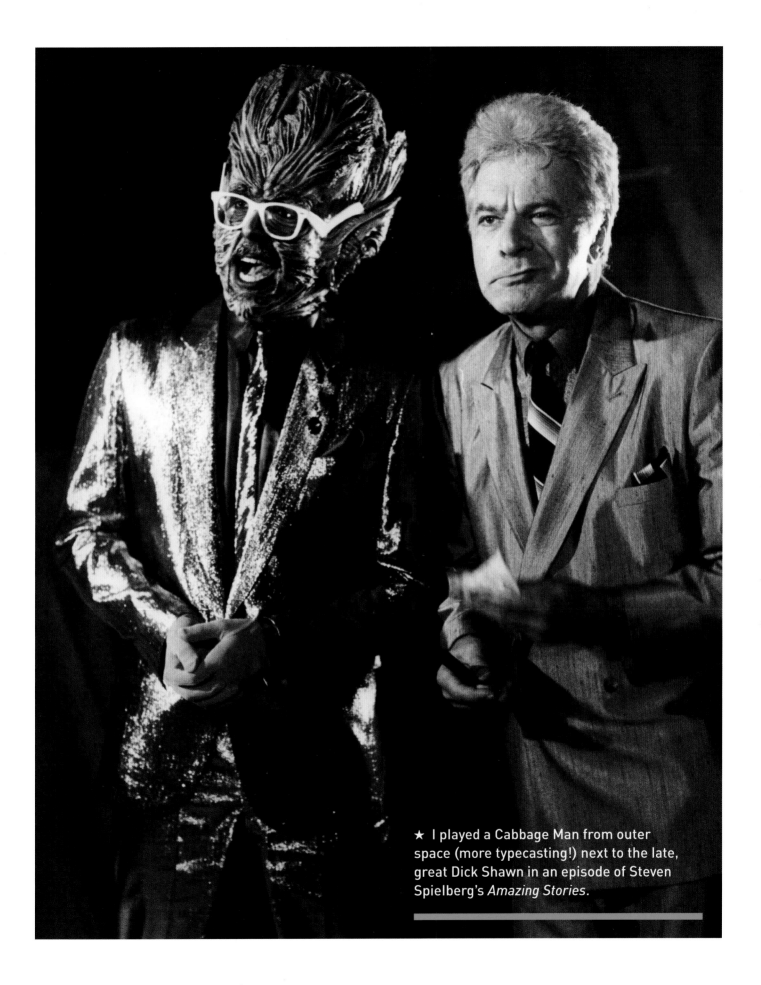

★ I played a Cabbage Man from outer space (more typecasting!) next to the late, great Dick Shawn in an episode of Steven Spielberg's *Amazing Stories*.

W
TWEET

SPOILER ALERT:
Unrefrigerated milk
goes bad quickly.

parodies was palpable. Though Al's singles would generally tackle the ubiquitous pop-culture phenomena everyone was familiar with, Al's idiosyncratic, offbeat, obsessive, and eclectic taste in music would shine through in original compositions that paid homage to superstars like R.E.M. but also to cult acts like Sparks, Oingo Boingo, Frank Zappa, and They Might Be Giants.

What other hugely popular mainstream artist would record not one but *two* tributes to New Wave obscurity Tonio K.? Children who bought Al's albums for the hits risked accidentally picking up a broad-ranging musical education in artists, songs, and styles they might never otherwise have been exposed to. If they weren't careful, they just might learn something.

Alas, it appeared that Al had taken *too* many chances on *Polka Party!,* which all backfired commercially. In this period of crisis and self-doubt, Yankovic returned to a familiar source of inspiration. He went with the closest thing there was to a sure thing in his life and career: a food-themed Michael Jackson parody.

If *Polka Party!* was mired by a level of miscalculation

★ Sam Emerson, Michael Jackson's personal photographer at the time, took all the pictures of me in the iconic buckle suit.

★ "Fat" by Derek Deal

FAT

Parody of "Bad" by MICHAEL JACKSON

New lyrics by AL YANKOVIC

Your butt is wide . . . well, mine is, too
Just watch your mouth . . . or I'll sit on you
The word is out . . . better treat me right
'Cause I'm the king . . . of cellulite
Ham on, ham on . . . ***ham on whole wheat . . .***
   all right

My zippers bust . . . my buckles break
I'm too much man . . . for you to take
The pavement cracks . . . when I fall down
I've got more chins . . . than Chinatown

Well, I never used a phone booth
And I never seen my toes
When I'm goin' to the movies
I take up seven rows

Because I'm fat, I'm fat, come on
You know I'm fat, I'm fat, you know it
You know I'm fat, I'm fat, come on, you know
Don't you call me pudgy, portly or stout
Just tell me once again, ***who's fat?***

When I walk out. . . to get my mail
It measures on . . . the Richter scale
Down at the beach . . . I'm a lucky man
I'm the only one . . . who gets a tan
If I have one more . . . pie á la mode
I'm gonna need . . . my own zip code

When you're only having seconds
I'm having twenty-thirds
When I go to get my shoes shined
I gotta take their word

Because I'm fat, I'm fat, come on
You know I'm fat, I'm fat, you know it
You know I'm fat, I'm fat, you know it, you know
And my shadow weighs forty-two pounds
Lemme tell you once again, who's fat . . .

If you see me comin' your way
Better give me plenty space
If I tell you that I'm hungry
Then won't you feed my face

Because I'm fat, I'm fat, come on
You know I'm fat, I'm fat, you know it
You know I'm fat, I'm fat, you know it, you know
When I sit around the house I really sit around the house
You know I'm fat, I'm fat, come on
You know I'm fat, I'm fat, you know it, you know it
You know, you know, you know, come on
And you know all by myself I'm a crowd
Lemme tell you once again . . .
You know I'm huge, I'm fat, you know it
You know I'm fat, you know, hoo!
You know I'm fat, I'm fat, you know it, you know
And the whole world knows I'm fat and I'm proud
Just tell me once again, who's fat?

★ During the shooting of the "Fat" video, I underwent four hours of prosthetic makeup every morning. (When I'm not doing a video shoot, it's only three.)

TWEET

"Please continue to hold—Your call is VERY important to us." Yeah, I can totally detect the sarcasm there, Staples.

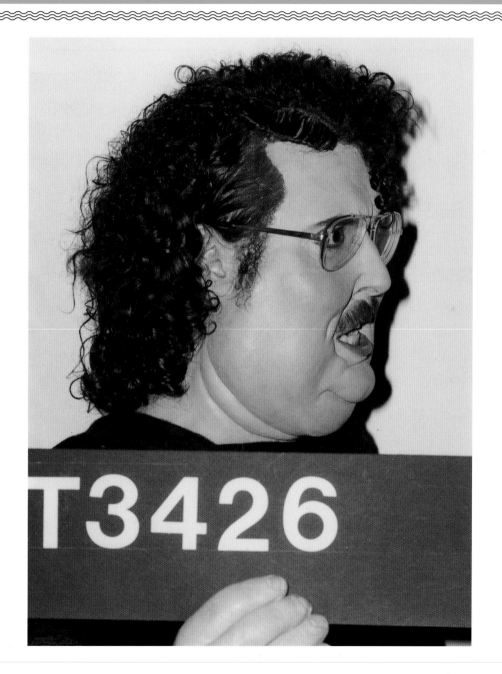

★ We took over a real store in Tulsa, Oklahoma, and turned it into Spatula City for the filming of *UHF*. In fact, there was an actual billboard for Spatula City off a freeway exit that stayed up for *months*.

seldom seen in Yankovic's oeuvre, his next album, *Even Worse*, illustrated that his gift for balancing the desires of a large mainstream audience with the dictates of his own idiosyncratic imagination remained unparalleled. "Fat," a parody of Michael Jackson's "Bad," was the massive MTV smash that helped make *Even Worse* Yankovic's first platinum hit. But there was more to *Even Worse* than fat jokes.

The Yankovic original "Melanie" illustrates Al's Warren Zevon and Randy Newman–like gift for smug-

★ Here's the cast of *UHF*, most of whom are now either dead or certifiably insane.

gling incredibly dark character studies of obsession into incongruously chipper, upbeat packages. "Melanie" could have been a gorgeous, old-fashioned doo-wop song if the unreliable narrator singing it weren't clearly insane. "Good Old Days," another Yankovic original, goes even further, pairing a nap-inducingly mellow folk arrangement and an AM-radio air of bland nostalgia to a narrative involving a young man who begins by torturing small animals before graduating to arson, torture, and mass

murder. Everybody knows the singles, but when it comes to Al, the deep cuts tend to be deeply demented.

Michael Jackson had once again proven Al's benefactor. But in 1988 Yankovic's mind was preoccupied by one area of the entertainment industry where Jackson hadn't yet dominated: film. After years of false starts and rejections, Al finally got a big green light from Orion Pictures and headed down to Tulsa, Oklahoma, to film

TWEET

Astronomers in Greenwich have recently determined that a "cotton pickin' minute" is actually 60.14978 seconds.

his starring and writing debut, *UHF*. Jay Levey directed and co-wrote.

UHF cast Yankovic as an inveterate daydreamer and underachiever named George who becomes the unlikely program director of a struggling UHF channel his degenerate gambler uncle had won in a card game. The dreamer turns the station's fortunes around through unconventional programming, like a kiddie show hosted by an eccentric janitor

★ The "UHF" music video was my most ambitious (and expensive) one up to that point, due to the numerous sets and costumes. My band appeared in a dozen incarnations, including the Beatles (left), Guns N' Roses (above), and ZZ Top (next page).

played by a pre-*Seinfeld* Michael Richards. In the process, the young upstart George makes a very powerful enemy in the director of a rival television channel, played with lip-smacking brio by the great character actor Kevin McCarthy of *Invasion of the Body Snatchers* cult fame.

Al and Jay had patterned the crucial role of Stanley, the spastic, demented janitor after Christopher Lloyd's Reverend Jim from *Taxi*. The young filmmakers had actually

considered Lloyd before ultimately offering the role to Richards. Al and Jay were blown away by the wiry actor's oddball delivery and unnerving commitment to character but were confused when Richards wavered about whether to accept the role. Richards eventually brought to Stanley both the manic physicality of a young Jerry Lewis and an air of being genuinely unhinged.

Al proved a generous lead, happy to defer to the demonic magnetism of Richards in the role that would have been career-defining were it not for that wacky-neighbor gig he played on that sitcom a few years later.

UHF can be seen as a cinematic extension of Al's beloved *Dr. Demento Show*. In *UHF*, as on *Dr. Demento*, the lunatics were running the asylum and smuggling vaudevillian subversion onto the airwaves. *UHF* was kooky. It was endearing. In the eyes of the studio execs at Orion, alas, it was viewed as the film that was going to save a troubled studio on the brink of extinction.

Why? *UHF* had the peculiar misfortune to score some of the highest ratings in focus-group testing of any Orion film since its unexpected 1987 blockbuster *Robocop*. As Al notes dryly, it's remarkable how much stock a studio puts in the opinions of a handful of twelve-year-olds in New Jersey.

When Orion looked at the test scores for *UHF*, cartoon dollar signs flashed in their eyes. They were

★ "UHF" by Tom Whalen

★ "UHF" by Todd Slater

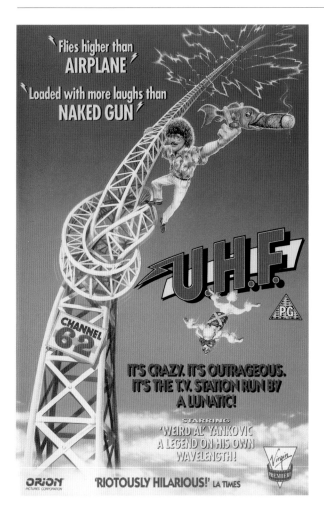

despite featuring guitar work by Dire Straits frontman Mark Knopfler himself.

Yankovic had already achieved more than he ever could have dreamed possible. He'd won Grammys. He'd released multiple gold albums. *Even Worse* had gone platinum. He'd become a household name. He'd delivered definitive parodies of Madonna, the Police, and Michael Jackson (twice). He'd appeared, bewildered and overwhelmed, on Japanese television. He'd cowritten and starred in a theatrically released motion picture.

Al's career had always been the longest of long shots. Had Al gone as far as his talent and work ethic would take him? Even he had to wonder if the ride was over. Orion had once looked at Al and saw the next Woody Allen. He was going to be their guy. They treated him like a movie star and filled his life with honeyed promises and platters of strawberries. Then *UHF* grossed just over two million dollars in its opening weekend and the strawberries disappeared and the honeyed promises turned to cold glares.

In a sense, Orion was right to have put their confidence in *UHF*. They were right to see it as a funny, charming, winning little sleeper that would go on to find an appreciative audience. In 1989, however, that audience was a little distracted by more high-profile fare that was competing with *UHF* for the attention of its core audience, underdogs with names like *Batman; Ghostbusters II; Honey, I Shrunk the Kids;* and *Lethal Weapon 2*. Orion had all the confidence in the world in *UHF*'s commercial potential. It turned out they had altogether too much confidence. Al's career as a cinematic leading man seemingly began and ended in the same sad weekend.

convinced they had the next sleeper blockbuster on their hands. There was talk of sequels and other Al vehicles until the first week's gross came in. Those ecstatic test scores began to seem like a bad joke. *UHF* wasn't a giant flop—its budget was too cheap for that—but it was slipping in and out of theaters in a hurry. The title didn't help, especially when it was inexplicably changed from *UHF* to *The Vidiot from UHF* in the Australian market.

Al didn't even have the comfort of a hit soundtrack album to console him. The album's confusingly titled single "Money for Nothing/Beverly Hillbillies" (much like *The Vidiot from UHF*, "The Beverly Hillbillies" was a hideous hybrid title foisted on him by jittery lawyers that made no one happy, Al least of all) went nowhere commercially

CHAPTER 3

KURT COBAIN

saves

ROCK & ROLL

and also

AL'S CAREER

AL NEVER ENTERED A BRIAN WILSON-ESQUE PERIOD OF SOUL-SHAKING DEPRESSION AND SAND-LADEN SELF-DOUBT BUT HE WAS FORCED TO RE-EXAMINE HIS LIFE AND HIS CAREER. The failure of *UHF* particularly stung, since Al had turned down the opportunity to open for Michael Jackson on the European leg of his tour in order to make the movie. Losing a sweet gig like that was bad enough; losing it for a brutal professional disappointment made it even worse.

Our hero was reeling from the failure of *UHF* and its soundtrack. In a state of mild panic, he returned once more to the tried and true. Terrified the entertainment industry wouldn't afford him many more chances if he landed another flop, Al went with the safest possible choice for his next single. Having scored smashes with the food-themed Michael Jackson parodies "Eat It" and "Fat," Yankovic shamelessly contemplated dipping into the well a third time with "Snack All Night," a parody of Jackson's latest message song, "Black or White."

It was, dear reader, the wrong parody at the wrong time. Even worse, it reeked of desperation. Deep down, Yankovic understood this. And so did Michael Jackson. Jackson had made Yankovic's career by saying yes to a parody of "Beat It." Jackson very well might have saved Al's career—or at least prevented him from making a very bad mistake—by saying no to a "Black or White" parody on the grounds that he didn't want to trivialize the song's socially conscious message. Jackson was doing Al an enormous favor. He was saving him from his worst instincts. "Snack All Night" was not going to happen. Al's professional future was a giant question mark.

★ When I met Samuel Bayer, the director of the "Smells Like Teen Spirit" video, he told me this was his favorite gag in "Smells Like Nirvana": the little person doing the low-angle lighting effects.

★ We shot at the same location and were able to get many of the same extras (including the cheerleaders and janitor) who appeared in the original Nirvana video. Fun trivia: one of the extras was skateboarding legend Tony Hawk!

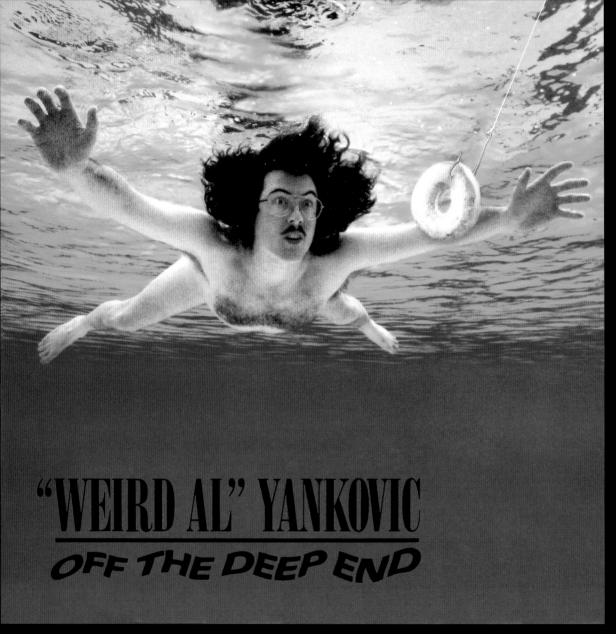

"WEIRD AL" YANKOVIC
OFF THE DEEP END

★ Thanks for asking, but no, I was not really naked in the pool. In fact, originally I never even intended to *appear* naked. I was wearing Hawaiian-print swim trunks for the shoot. But after studying the contact sheets, I found myself liking the shots where my body was twisted in a way that you couldn't *tell* I was wearing trunks. So we went with one of the "naked" pictures.

 TWEET | I just watched *Source Code* on DVD—it all seemed completely believable until I saw Jake Gyllenhaal using Bing as his search engine.

Then in the early '90s a beautiful, misunderstood loner from Seattle named Kurt Cobain saved Al's career and also rock and roll with a set of power chords and intriguingly enigmatic, mumbled lyrics. He single-handedly brought a dying art form roaring back to life via a paradigmshifting single called "Smells Like Teen Spirit."

This was Elvis on *The Ed Sullivan Show*. This was Hendrix at Woodstock. This was Johnny Rotten sneering about the queen. More pointedly, this was Michael Jackson cementing his legend by moonwalking on *Motown 25*. This was pop-culture history in the making. Al could feel the ground beneath him shifting. This was important. This mattered. This was the cultural moment that Al

had been waiting for. Al once again had a date with the cultural zeitgeist.

When it came to parodying "Smells Like Teen Spirit," Al had another huge advantage: he loved the song. And the singer-songwriter. And the album. This wasn't just a hit song for him to parody; this was music that spoke to him. This wasn't a flash in the pan like Gerardo enjoying his fifteen minutes of fame with "Rico Suave"; this was a genius making a statement as cryptic as it was important.

Beyond that, Kurt Cobain was funny. He got it. His generation-defining anthem was named after a *deodorant* and contained lyrics that deliberately defied literal understanding. Is it any wonder this strange, glorious young

HOUSEHOLD HINTS

You can remove unsightly blemishes with an ordinary cheese grater.

Did you know that if you ever run out of shaving cream, warm Velveeta is a quick and easy replacement?

Fun breakfast idea: cut a big hole out of the middle of your toast, and fill it with pie!

You can use lemon juice to get the goat's blood out of the drapes.

At any moment, day or night, a meteorite could cave your skull right in. Always, always, ALWAYS wear a helmet.

man was a big Weird Al fan and found the prospect of Al spoofing one of his songs incredibly flattering? The time was right. The pairing of seeming opposites was perfect: pop music's Mr. Clean and its preeminent dark and tormented hero.

There is no truer benediction for a newly minted pop star than a parody from Weird Al. Kurt Cobain and Nirvana had arrived. And they'd accidentally resurrected Al's career in the process. Just as Al's love for Devo and Talking Heads had informed every note of "Dare to Be Stupid" and "Dog Eat Dog" respectively, "Smells Like Nirvana" was a big-hearted valentine to Nirvana thinly disguised as a spoof.

Off the Deep End's track listing reflected the strange cultural moment that birthed it—1992. Yankovic's loving tribute to a band that would change music forever shared space with parodies of instantly dated featherweights like Gerardo ("Taco Grande"), MC Hammer ("I Can't Watch This") and New Kids on the Block ("The White Stuff").

Aside from "Smells Like Nirvana," *Off the Deep End*'s masterpiece and most enduring hit is "You Don't Love Me Anymore"—a Yankovic original. It's the musical equivalent of a heart-shaped Whitman's Valentine Sampler stocked with arsenic-laced chocolates—a sweet-sounding quasi-ballad that grows more disturbing and morose with each line as Al ponders losing the waning affection of a girlfriend whose hostility toward the narrator almost invariably takes the form of murder attempts.

Off the Deep End wasn't just the album that saved Al's career. It was also the first album Al produced himself. Yankovic had enormous respect for his longtime producer, Rick Derringer, but he was discovering that no one could realize his perfectionist vision for his music like he could. That extended to his music videos. Yankovic's successful stint as a music-video star in the '80s had doubled as a rough apprenticeship during which Al, the eternal student, learned and mastered the technical and creative components of directing music videos. As a director, Al had obvious strengths. He possessed a clear creative vision for each video and was adept at making the most of a tiny budget, especially where special effects and animation were concerned.

★ Out of all the surrealistic moments in my life, being on *Wheel of Fortune* with James Brown and Little Richard is definitely in the top ten.

YOU DON'T LOVE ME

ANYMORE

by AL YANKOVIC

We've been together for so very long

But now things are changing,

oh I wonder what's wrong?

Seems you don't want me around

The passion is gone and the flame's died down

I guess I lost a little bit of self-esteem

That time that you made it with the whole hockey team

You used to think I was nice

Now you tell all your friends that I'm the Antichrist

Oh, why did you disconnect the brakes on my car?

That kind of thing is hard to ignore

Got a funny feeling

You don't love me anymore

I knew that we were having problems when

You put those piranhas in my bathtub again

You're still the light of my life

Oh, darlin', I'm beggin', won't you put down that knife?

You know I even think it's kinda cute the way

You poison my coffee just a little each day

I still remember the way that you laughed

When you pushed me down the elevator shaft

Oh, if you don't mind me askin', what's this poisonous cobra

Doin' in my underwear drawer?

Sometimes I get to thinking

You don't love me anymore

You slammed my face down on the barbecue grill

Now my scars are all healing but my heart never will

You set my house on fire

You pulled out my chest hairs with an old pair of pliers

Oh, you think I'm ugly and you say I'm cheap

You shaved off my eyebrows
while I was asleep

You drilled a hole in my head

Then you dumped me in a drainage ditch and left me for dead

Oh, you know this really isn't like you at all

You never acted this way before

Honey, something tells me

You don't love me anymore

Oh no, no

Got a funny feeling
You don't love me anymore

★ "Smells Like Nirvana" by Dave Perillo

★ At one point I wanted to do a ridiculously out-of-character glamour shot like this for one of my album covers, but—perhaps fortunately—I was talked out of it. A similar shot was used for the inside cover of the *Alapalooza* booklet.

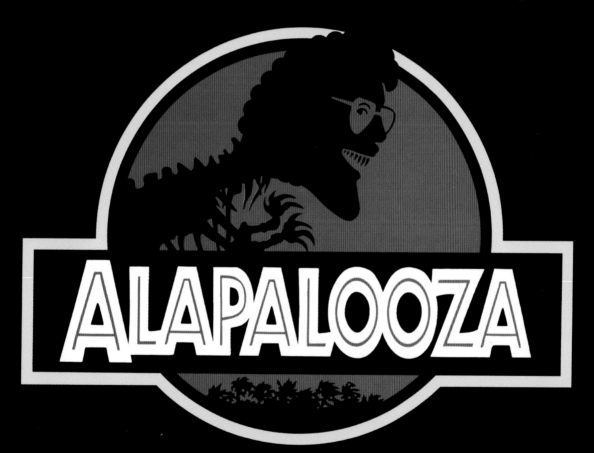

★ On the set of the "Bedrock Anthem" video (in the middle of nowhere) with Jay Levey. This was my first time directing a big-budget music video, and it was kind of nerve-wracking. As this was the pre-laptop era, you can see me working out of the same 3-ring binder with plastic tab dividers that I'd had since high school.

 TWEET | My 8-year-old daughter totally fell asleep at the table during dinner last night. That girl can NOT hold her alcohol.

Al was so innately gifted as a music-video director that soon he wasn't just directing his own attention-grabbing videos. He was also directing videos for fans and colleagues like the Jon Spencer Blues Explosion, Hanson, the Black Crowes, the Presidents of the United States of America, and his good buddy Ben Folds, who would eventually contribute a piano track to Al's brilliant pastiche of Folds's work, "Why Does This Always Happen to Me?"

The hits kept coming. But Al wasn't about to wait for a hit song to again capture the cultural zeitgeist.

★ After a scene-stealing cameo in "Smells Like Nirvana," I had no choice but to ask Dick Van Patten back so that he could also be horribly out of place in the "Bedrock Anthem" video.

For the first single off his 1993 album *Alapalooza,* Yankovic cross-pollinated a beloved old chestnut from years past—"MacArthur Park"—with the biggest cinematic phenomenon of the year, *Jurassic Park. Alapalooza* found Al in a prehistoric state of mind; along with Al's tongue-in-cheek homage to Steven Spielberg's dinosaur movie, the album spawned the *Flintstones*-themed Red Hot Chili Peppers spoof "Bedrock Anthem."

Yankovic was once again in tune with the times, yet the album's most resonant tracks were defiantly untimely. The R.E.M. pastiche "Frank's 2000 TV"

BURNING QUESTIONS THAT KEEP ME UP ALL NIGHT

If they can put a man on the moon, why can't they put a koala on the moon?

Was Red Skelton ever bitter about not being invited into Sinatra's Rat Pack?

What would Joseph Stalin have done for a Klondike bar?

Is it OK for vegetarians to eat tofu nut loaf from a bowl made out of a monkey's skull?

When exactly does "The Ice Cream of the Future" become "The Ice Cream of the Present"?

★ I'll never be able to repay Dr. Demento for everything he's done for me, but as a small token of my appreciation, just because I know it means a lot to him, every Sunday afternoon in the park I give him a piggyback ride.

  I just explained to my daughter that rain is actually cloud pee. That's accurate, right?

is perhaps the prettiest song Al has ever written, as well as an unusually pure and insightful reflection of his eternal love-hate relationship with pop culture and technology. "Young, Dumb & Ugly" takes the snotty outlaw posturing of AC/DC to surreal, pointless, and nonsensical levels; the clueless narrator takes altogether too much pride in undertipping a waitress in lieu of more genuinely transgressive acts.

Al has earned a reputation as one of the nicest men in show business. Though the first amend-

★ Every now and then I make a pilgrimage to Darwin, Minnesota, just to snuggle up to the world-famous twine ball.

ment protects parody and satire as free speech, Al has always gone the extra step and requested permission from both the artists he parodies and their respective labels. This serves multiple purposes. It helps ensure that Al doesn't make enemies unnecessarily and it lends an "official" quality to Al's spoofs.

So Al was shocked to discover that Coolio claimed Yankovic's "Amish Paradise," his parody of "Gangsta's Paradise" on 1996's *Bad Hair Day*, had "desecrated" his original and was

disrespectful in its depiction of the Amish way of life. A
man seemingly without enemies suddenly found himself
embroiled in a silly, one-sided feud when Coolio claimed
never to have given Yankovic permission to parody his
song. The two later resolved their differences amicably.

★ A decade after "Amish Paradise," I bumped
into Coolio at a trade show in Las Vegas and
we hugged it out. Water under the bridge.

Bad Hair Day also contained one of Al's most over-
looked and underrated gems, a gleefully absurd tribute
to fellow musical funnymen They Might Be Giants called
"Everything You Know Is Wrong." On a bleaker note,
the album also featured "The Night Santa Went Crazy," a
Yuletide number so dark it makes "Christmas at Ground
Zero" sound like "Silver Bells" by comparison.

There was clearly only one place left to go for the
sick soul behind "Christmas at Ground Zero" and "The
Night Santa Went Crazy": Saturday morning children's
television. Al and Jay had discussed making the move to

★ It's often been said that I'm out standing in my field, and here I am proving it.

AMISH PARADISE

Parody of "Gangsta's Paradise" by COOLIO

New lyrics by AL YANKOVIC

As I walk through the valley where I harvest my grain

I take a look at my wife and realize she's very plain

But that's just perfect for an Amish like me

You know I shun fancy things like electricity

At 4:30 in the morning I'm milkin' cows

Jebediah feeds the chickens and Jacob plows . . . fool

And I've been milkin' and plowin' so long that

Even Ezekiel thinks that my mind is gone

I'm a man of the land, I'm into discipline

Got a Bible in my hand and a beard on my chin

But if I finish all of my chores and you finish thine

Then ***tonight we're gonna party like it's 1699***

We been spending most our lives

Living in an Amish paradise

I've churned butter once or twice

Living in an Amish paradise

It's hard work and sacrifice

Living in an Amish paradise

We sell quilts at discount price

Living in an Amish paradise

A local boy kicked me in the butt last week

I just smiled at him and I turned the other cheek

I really don't care, in fact I wish him well

'Cause I'll be laughing my head off when he's burning in hell

But ***I ain't never punched a tourist***
even if he deserved it

An Amish with a 'tude? You know that's unheard of

I never wear buttons but I got a cool hat

And my homies agree I really look good in black . . . fool

If you come to visit, you'll be bored to tears

We haven't even paid the phone bill in 300 years

But we ain't really quaint, so please don't point and stare

We're just technologically impaired

There's ***no phone, no lights, no motorcar***

Not a single luxury

Like Robinson Crusoe

It's as primitive as can be

We been spending most our lives

Living in an Amish paradise

We're just plain and simple guys

Living in an Amish paradise

There's no time for sin and vice

Living in an Amish paradise

We don't fight, we all play nice

Living in an Amish paradise

Hitchin' up the buggy, churnin' lots of butter

Raised a barn on Monday,
soon I'll raise anutter

Think you're really righteous? Think you're pure in heart?

Well, I know I'm a million times as humble as thou art

I'm the pious guy the little Amlettes wanna be like

On my knees day and night scorin' points for the afterlife

So don't be vain and don't be whiny

Or else, my brother, I might have to get medieval on your heinie

We been spending most our lives

Living in an Amish paradise

We're all crazy Mennonites

Living in an Amish paradise

There's no cops or traffic lights

Living in an Amish paradise

But you'd probably think it bites

Living in an Amish paradise

★ "Than Thou Art" by Adam Hanson

TWEET

Didn't see anybody famous sitting in First Class. If this plane crashes, I am TOTALLY getting the headline!

★ I've worn these Coolio braids three times in my life: once for the album cover, once for the "Amish Paradise" video shoot, and once for when I was co-presenting with Coolio at the American Music Awards. I don't recommend them—they're *excruciatingly painful*.

I am advocating stronger legislation for turnip truck safety. Imagine how many people must have fallen off for that to become a cliché.

children's television since the mid-1980s and encountered plenty of stops and starts along the way before getting into business with Dick Clark Productions and CBS in the mid-1990s for what would become *The Weird Al Show.*

Al had high hopes for *The Weird Al Show.* This was an opportunity to do a kids' show with integrity, a show that would respect children's intelligence and never talk down to them. Al dreamed of getting all his heroes involved. He dreamed of luring the reclusive Tom Lehrer back into the spotlight to play a mysterious character known only as the Guy Boarded in the Wall before ultimately casting Eddie Deezen in the role. He convinced his hero Stan Freberg to accept recurring guest roles. One of the biggest regrets in Al's life and career, however, was that he never took the great Shel Silverstein up on

★ Taking a break on the set of "Gump" with Pat Boone, Ruth Buzzi (as her *Laugh-In* character Gladys Ormphby), and Andy Comeau (as Forrest Gump).

his offer to serve as an unofficial adviser—a Yoda to Al's Luke Skywalker—on the new show after a chance meeting in a record store.

Al assembled a murderer's row of talent for his new show. For the announcer, he snagged *Ren & Stimpy* and *Futurama* voice artist Billy West. Peyton Reed, who would go on to direct *Bring It On* and *Down with Love,* helmed the show, and future *Arrested Development* and *30 Rock* writer Ron Weiner was part of a small but accomplished writing staff overseen by the perennially hands-on Al, who served as head writer as well as star, creator, and co-executive producer.

Al had a beautiful set created by Wayne White, the same genius who had helped create the brilliant set for *Pee-wee's Playhouse.* He had talented collaborators, a clear vision, and good intentions. It is wise to remember at this point, dear reader, that the nature trail to hell is paved with good intentions. The project was soon inundated with something much more sinister than that, as far as Al was concerned: notes from executives at CBS.

Al and his collaborators were shocked both by what the network objected to—the word "barbarians," for example—and what the network allowed: depictions of gambling; a parody of an educational film that featured stomach-churning footage of diseased teeth; and show after show of Al behaving like a selfish, self-absorbed jerk desperately in need of a government-mandated life lesson every week.

★ While shooting the opening title sequence for the movie *Spy Hard*, I had to sing underwater, spin through the air while connected to crotch-torturing wires (pictured here), and ultimately *get my head blown up*.

★ Even though *The Weird Al Show* aired on CBS, it was shot at NBC, across the hall from Jay Leno. In fact, we shot it on the very stage where Johnny Carson had done *The Tonight Show*.

 TWEET I always drive in the diamond lane, because I think it's fair to count the microscopic organisms living on my skin as passengers.

The network's increasingly nonsensical insistence that Al's labor of love meet the "educational" demands of the FCC drove *The Weird Al Show* to conduct passive-aggressive experiments in revenge on the clueless suits. In a none-too-subtle indication of how the show *really* felt about the ham-fisted messages they were forced to impart, the "lesson" of the day was presented at the beginning of each episode, then ripped violently apart.

The Weird Al Show succeeded in subverting and spoofing the social messages it was being strong-armed into delivering, but fighting to preserve his vision of a *Mr. Show* for kids or a musical *Pee-wee's Playhouse* exacted a toll on Al

★ Wayne White was the production and set designer for *Pee-wee's Playhouse*, as well as *The Weird Al Show*. My show was actually similar to Pee-wee's in many ways, except, you know, in popularity and success.

★ For a while, everywhere I went, I brought a fifty-foot-tall inflatable replica of myself with me. Is that so wrong?

★ A publicity shot from *The Weird Al Show*.
I wonder who wound up with this chair?

You know the old saying: "Go to bed covered in honey, wake up covered in ants"? I tried it—it's totally accurate!!

TWEET

physically and psychologically. Al had never been one to shy away from a challenge or hard work. On the contrary, he's always been the type to race madly *toward* a challenge and hard work. But even he had to feel daunted by the prospect of creating, starring in, executive-producing, and being head writer on a show that had inexplicably been hijacked by the morals police and transformed into a cynical attempt to conform to well-intentioned but ultimately ill-considered new government regulations.

The network didn't want Al to slyly Trojan-horse nice messages into a funny and irreverent kids' show. They wanted Al to beat children over the head with the most obvious, insultingly heavy-handed "lessons" imaginable so that it could stay on the good side of the FCC. CBS didn't care if they ruined the delicate alchemy of Al's show in the process.

Accordingly, the audio commentary for the series, which was released on DVD by Shout Factory in 2006 after the show had picked up a fierce cult following among Al fans, is filled with gallows humor, dark comedy, and the kind of hard-bitten camaraderie more often seen in men who fought in a proper war together rather than a series of skirmishes with clueless network yes-men.

Al had had dreams. Big plans. Visions of being able to choose between Aerosmith and U2 as the show's weekly musical guest. He ended up being grateful that alt-rock non-entity Radish was able to clear time off their schedule to appear on national television.

The Weird Al Show was supposed to have been the logical next step in Al's career. Instead it was a Kafkaesque nightmare that threatened to destroy the souls of everyone involved, especially Al. CBS never seemed to know what to do with the show. It even gave *The Weird Al Show* a lead-in that might not be the best possible fit for a delightful exercise in mirth and merriment: the morning news.

Yet Al and his talented collaborators soldiered on regardless, turning out a show that even in its compromised form reflects Al's wonderfully warped mind. Though some of Al's more outré ideas were nixed by the network—such as having a character named "Bobby the Inquisitive Boy" be played by a different actor every episode without ever acknowledging or explaining the change—plenty of absurd, challenging, and agreeably insane ideas made the cut, from a faux-commercial for a pizza place that saves valuable seconds by removing boxes from the equation to a creepily narcotized kids'-show host reviled by his contemptuous puppet sidekicks.

Though Al jokes on the audio commentary that the inherent contradictions of trying to reconcile his own idiosyncratic sensibility with the over-the-top demands of delivering an "educational" show rendered *The Weird Al Show* a "show for nobody," he drastically underrates the show's quality and appeal. Compromised or not, *The Weird Al Show* more than lives up to the exceedingly high, exacting standards Al had set for every other aspect of his career. It's funny, smart, and, if anything, rendered even stranger by the network's meddling.

CHAPTER 4

A NEW LOOK AL *for a* NEW ERA

★ "Sorry girls, he's married!"

BY THE TIME *THE WEIRD AL SHOW* ENDED ITS BRIEF BUT GLORIOUS RUN IN DECEMBER 1997, AL HAD DEVELOPED SUCH A STRIKING PERSONA THAT HE COULD BE RECOGNIZED JUST FROM HIS SILHOUETTE.

Hawaiian shirts, a bushy mustache, and geeky glasses were the hallmarks of one of the most instantly recognized personas in all of entertainment. Looking weird had reaped huge dividends for Al. It worked. Why mess with success?

But Al did the unthinkable: he shaved off his mustache. Then he did the even more unthinkable: he got LASIK surgery to correct his vision. Back in 1983's video for "Ricky," a clean-shaven and pompadour-sporting Al made for a shockingly convincing Ricky Ricardo. In every video after that, however, Al was essentially choosing to share creative DNA with the artists he covered, parodying their look as well as their music. The effect was like the genetic joining of Jeff Goldblum and a winged

★ *Simpsons* creator Matt Groening came to my show one time when I played my alma mater Cal Poly—and he even dressed up for it!

insect in *The Fly*. So instead of Kurt Cobain we got a Weird Al/Kurt Cobain hybrid—half geek, half grunge. Al enjoyed disappearing into characters, and he was finding it hard to be a chameleon with something as distinctive as a glasses-mustache combo.

The classic Weird Al look is so burned into the cultural consciousness, however, that when fans dress up like Al for Halloween—and plenty of them do—they almost invariably choose the scruffy, old-look Al over the sleeker contemporary version. It's not that fans rejected Al's new look as much as they were unwilling to completely give up the Al they grew up with. Weird Al fandom is handed down from generation to generation. Buying a Weird Al album has been a rite of passage for young people

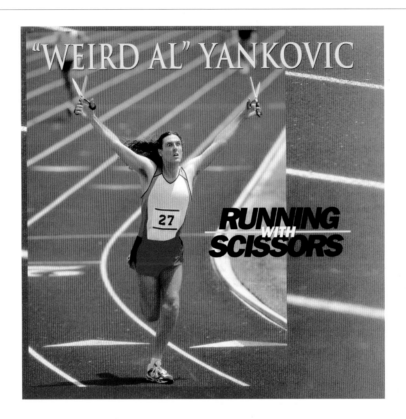

TWEET

Just walked 2 whole blocks and didn't see a single Starbucks. Where am I, Communist China??

since the '80s. Geeks, outsiders, brainiacs, and misfits all looked at Al and saw themselves. In the '80s and '90s he was the epitome of a figure that would soon transform our culture and society: the triumphant geek, the nerd as world-beater. In the past decade, he's loomed as a respected elder statesman of geekdom, both in music and in what is nebulously called the alternative comedy world.

In the '80s, Al's music obsessed about food. He

★ This was the hardest I ever had to work for an album cover. I had to sprint at full speed several dozen times so that the photographer could capture the perfect moment.

couldn't help it; it was all he ate. As time marched on and Al relied on his own knack for being ahead of the curve culturally, Al and Jon became obsessed with computers—long before they became ubiquitous. Jon built Al a snazzy website he runs to this day, and Al's obsession with all things digital began to slip into his songs. For example, on "It's All About the Pentiums" from 1999's *Running with Scissors*, Al appropriated Sean "Diddy" Combs's

IT'S ALL ABOUT THE PENTIUMS

Parody of "It's All About the Benjamins" by PUFF DADDY & THE FAMILY

New lyrics by AL YANKOVIC

It's all about the Pentiums, baby

Uhh

Uh-huh, yeah

Uhh

Uh-huh, yeah

It's all about the Pentiums, baby . . . Uhh

It's all about the Pentiums, baby . . . Uh-huh, yeah

It's all about the Pentiums, baby . . . Uhh

It's all about the Pentiums, baby

What y'all wanna do?

Wanna be hackers? Code crackers? Slackers

Wastin' time with all the chatroom yakkers?

9 to 5, chillin' at Hewlett Packard?

Workin' at a desk with a dumb little placard?

Yeah, payin' the bills with my mad programming skills

Defraggin' my hard drive for thrills

I got me a hundred gigabytes of RAM

I never feed trolls and I don't read spam

Installed a T1 line in my house

***Always at my* PC,**

double-clickin' on my mizouse

Upgrade my system at least twice a day

I'm strictly plug-and-play, I ain't afraid of Y2K

I'm down with Bill Gates, I call him Money for short

I phone him up at home and I make him do my tech support

It's all about the Pentiums, what?

You gotta be the dumbest newbie I've ever seen

You've got white-out all over your screen

You think your Commodore 64 is really neato

What kinda chip you got in there, a Dorito?

You're usin' a 286? Don't make me laugh

Your Windows boots up in what, a day and a half?

You could back up your whole hard drive

ON A FLOPPY DISKETTE

You're the biggest joke on the Internet
Your database is a disaster
You're waxin' your modem, tryin' to make it go faster
Hey fella, I bet you're still livin' in your parents' cellar
Downloadin' pictures of Sarah Michelle Gellar
And postin' "Me too!" like some brain-dead AOL-er
I should do the world a favor and cap you like Old Yeller
You're just about as useless as jpegs to Helen Keller

It's all about the Pentiums!
It's all about the Pentiums!
It's all about the Pentiums!
It's all about the Pentiums!
Now, what y'all wanna do?

Wanna be hackers? Code crackers? Slackers

Wastin' time with all the chatroom yakkers?
9 to 5, chillin' at Hewlett Packard?

Wanna run wit my crew, hah?
Rule cyberspace and crunch numbers like I do?

They call me the king of the spreadsheets

Got 'em all printed out on my bed sheets
My new computer's got the clocks, it rocks
But it was obsolete before I opened the box
You say you've had your desktop for over a week?
Throw that junk away, man, it's an antique!
Your laptop is a month old? Well, that's great
If you could use a nice, heavy paperweight
My digital media is write-protected
Every file inspected, no viruses detected

It's all about
THE PENTIUMS, BABY

I beta tested every operating system
Gave props to some, and others? I dissed 'em
While your computer's crashin', mine's multitaskin'
It does all my work without me even askin'
Got a flat-screen monitor, 40" wide
I believe that yours says "Etch-A-Sketch" on the side
In a 32-bit world, you're a 2-bit user
You've got your own newsgroup, alt.total-loser
Your motherboard melts when you try to send a fax

Where'd you get your CPU, in a box of Cracker Jacks?

Play me online? Well, you know that I'll beat you
If I ever meet you I'll control-alt-delete you
What?

It's all about the Pentiums!
It's all about the Pentiums!
It's all about the Pentiums!
It's all about the Pentiums!
What y'all wanna do?
Wanna be hackers? Code crackers? Slackers
Wastin' time with all the chatroom yakkers?
9 to 5, chillin' at Hewlett Packard?
What?

★ Listening back to a mix from the *Straight Outta Lynwood* sessions (Westlake Audio, studio E).

MILLION DOLLAR IDEAS

They really should make Sextuple Stuf Oreos. Six times the cream filling, plus, y'know . . . it sounds pretty *kinky*.

If I ever were to open up a store that sold nothing but bottled saliva, I'd definitely name it Great Expectorations.

Triumph the Insult Comic Dog needs an endorsement deal with Grey Poupon mustard. "Hey, that's a great sandwich . . . *for me to Poupon*!"

Encountering various wild animals in the forest: Make myself "big" or "small"? Need iPhone app!

I think televised golf would be more fun to watch if they had color commentary by that Hindenburg announcer guy.

★ True to form, we decided to do a teaser campaign for "The Saga Begins" that openly mocked the teaser campaign for *Star Wars: Episode 1*.

hoarse rasp to inhabit the character of an arrogant and incongruously aggressive computer geek.

Al was making other changes as well. When the producers of VH1's *Behind the Music* chronicled Al, they realized that his story tragically did not follow the "Meteoric rise/ nightmare descent into booze and pills/dramatic comeback" arc endemic to most rock mythology, so they decided to play up Al's one-sided beef with Coolio, as well as his supposed loneliness. In actuality, Al was perfectly happy as a single man, just as his future wife, Suzanne, was perfectly happy as a single woman. But they discovered they could be even happier as a couple, and they married in 2001. It was Bill Mumy, Al's old pal from the *Dr. Demento Show* days and *Lost in Space,* who had introduced Al and Suzanne, a beautiful, brilliant businesswoman. Al and Suzanne's joy was further amplified by the birth of their daughter, Nina, in 2003. An idol of children the world over now had a child himself.

Al was making changes in his professional as well as personal life. When Scotti

Brothers was liquidated in 1997, Al eventually ended up on the Sony label. The good folks over at Scotti Brothers had made Al feel like their children wouldn't get Christmas presents and they'd be forced to sell their clothing unless Al pumped out a hit album every year.

Sony, thankfully, was a little less dependent on Al. Nevertheless, Al was keeping his antennae finely tuned for a pop-culture phenomenon to transform into his next big smash. In the 1990s, Al had gravitated toward tongue-in-cheek odes to blockbusters. First he'd fused "MacArthur Park" with Steven Spielberg for the song "Jurassic Park." Then came "Gump," Al's goofy riff on the Presidents of the United States of America's "Lump" as well as the blockbuster movie *Forrest Gump.*

In the late '90s, Al had his sights set on spoofing the *Star Wars* prequel *The Phantom Menace* for the first single to his 1999 album *Running With Scissors.* There was just one small problem: the movie hadn't come out yet. And though the folks over at Lucasfilm loved Al, they

★ Queen Amidala was played by my first cousin once removed, Tammy Sidell. I like to cast my relatives in things—they have great attitudes, and they work cheap!

THE SAGA

BEGINS

Parody of "American Pie" by DON MCLEAN

New lyrics by AL YANKOVIC

A long, long time ago
In a galaxy far away

Naboo was under an attack

And I thought me and Qui-Gon Jinn

Could talk the Federation into

Maybe cutting them a little slack

But their response, it didn't thrill us

They locked the doors and tried to kill us

We escaped from that gas

Then met Jar Jar and Boss Nass

We took a bongo from the scene

And we went to Theed to see the queen

We all wound up on Tatooine
That's where we found this boy . . .

Oh my my, this here Anakin guy

May be Vader someday later, now he's just a small fry

And he left his home and kissed his mommy goodbye

Sayin' "Soon I'm gonna be a Jedi"

"Soon I'm gonna be a Jedi"

Did you know this junkyard slave
Isn't even old enough to shave

But he can use the Force, they say

Ahh, *do you see him hitting on the queen*

Though he's just nine and she's fourteen

Yeah, he's probably gonna marry her someday

Well, I know he built C-3PO

And I've heard how fast his pod can go

And we were broke, it's true

So we made a wager or two

He was a prepubescent flyin' ace

And the minute Jabba started off that race

Well, I knew who would win first place

Oh yes, it was our boy

We started singin' . . . My my, this here Anakin guy

May be Vader someday later, now he's just a small fry

And he left his home and kissed his
mommy goodbye

Sayin' "Soon I'm gonna be a **Jedi**"

"Soon I'm gonna be a Jedi"

Now we finally got to Coruscant

The Jedi Council we knew would want

To see how good the boy could be

So we took him there and we told the tale

How his midi-chlorians were off the scale

And he might fulfill that prophecy

Oh, the Council was impressed, of course

Could he bring balance to **the Force?**

They interviewed the kid

Oh, training they forbid

Because Yoda sensed in him much fear

And Qui-Gon said, "Now listen here

Just **stick it in your pointy ear**

I still will teach this boy"

He was singin' . . . My my, this here Anakin guy

May be Vader someday later, now he's just a small fry

And he left his home and kissed his mommy goodbye

Sayin' "Soon I'm gonna be a Jedi"

"Soon I'm gonna be a Jedi"

We caught a ride back to Naboo

'Cause Queen Amidala wanted to

I frankly would've liked to stay

We all fought in that epic war

And it wasn't long at all before

Little Hotshot flew his plane and saved the day

And in the end some Gungans died

Some ships blew up and some pilots fried

A lot of folks were croakin'

The battle droids were broken

And the Jedi I admire most

Met up with Darth Maul and now he's toast

Well, I'm still here and he's a ghost

I guess I'll train this boy

And I was singin' . . . My my, this here Anakin guy

May be Vader someday later, now he's just a small fry

And he left his home and kissed his mommy goodbye

Sayin' "Soon I'm gonna be a Jedi"

"Soon I'm gonna be a Jedi"

We were singin' . . . My my, this here Anakin guy

May be Vader someday later, now he's just a small fry

And he left his home and kissed his mommy goodbye

Sayin' ***"Soon I'm gonna be a Jedi"***

May be Vader someday later,

NOW HE'S JUST A SMALL FRY

SAGE ADVICE

"When life gives you turmeric, make coconut curry"—old East Indian saying I just made up.

Re: signing a contract with Satan— never use your own blood, just regular ink.

If the guy at Hertz Rent-a-Car asks if you want a Hertz donut, SAY NO.

Starbucks has a secret menu. If you order a "dirty chai latte" you get a non-fat chai latte with rat feces. Who knew?

Remember, always operate heavy machinery on drugs. (Or is it never? I forget, one of the two.)

★ The band posed on stage for this photo taken at the end of the 2000 tour, our busiest touring year ever (150 shows).

★ When we performed "Like a Surgeon" on stage in the '80s, we used to wheel out a female patient on a hospital gurney and cut her in half with a chain-saw. After Madonna's *Truth or Dare* movie came out, we segued to sexy dancing and cone bras.

When I'm on my deathbed, I'll probably look back at my life and think, "I should have tweeted more."

TWEET

guarded the plot details of the upcoming science-fiction blockbuster tenaciously.

Time was of the essence, so Al took another huge gamble and cobbled together a rough sense of the movie's plot from Internet rumors and determined rambles through cyberspace. Al's instincts and *Star Wars* super-fandom served him well. Without having seen the film or reading its script, he was nevertheless able to faithfully detail its premise for the single that would become "The Saga Begins." It was the kind of song only Al could pull off. He had to unpack a world of

★ On the set of the video for "The Saga Begins."

exposition and make the complicated plot of *The Phantom Menace* fit the loping, rambling rhythms of "American Pie" in a way that was organic, natural, and funny.

In 2003, nothing in pop culture was bigger than Eminem or his brilliant semi-autobiographical vehicle *8 Mile*. "Lose Yourself," the Oscar-winning underdog anthem from the *8 Mile* soundtrack, inspired Al to write another homage/parody of television addiction (in the vein of previous numbers like *Running With Scissors'* "Jerry Springer," *Dare To Be Stupid*'s "Cable TV," and *Polka Party*'s "Here's Johnny"),

★ After effectively being eliminated from Grammy competition for a decade (for a while the Comedy category was limited to spoken word only) it was enormously gratifying for me to come back and win Grammy number three for my album *Poodle Hat*.

TWEET I like to start every day by drinking a double espresso and punching a shark in the face.

★ "Weird Al" by Joshua Budich

★ I was thrilled to work with one of my favorite photographers, Mark Seliger, for the *Poodle Hat* session. Jim West was less than thrilled to wear that jacket.

which he titled "Couch Potato." Eminem was considerate enough to give Al permission to parody the song, but when it came time to film the music video, Eminem inexplicably decided that making a video would somehow compromise the original's artistic integrity. Eminem's actions seemed hypocritical, given that parodying pop stars had long been a cornerstone of his own videos. The first-amendment advocate and free-speech martyr was suddenly willing to draw a hard line at the world's most beloved parodist mildly spoofing his image and persona. Eminem could handle anything, apparently, besides gentle mockery.

Eminem's professional hissy fit played havoc with the commercial potential of one of Al's funniest and most insightful albums—2003's *Poodle Hat.* Another track on *Poodle Hat,* the Ben Folds homage "Why Does This Always Happen to Me?" amplifies the noxious self-absorption of the American character to hilarious extremes. The soulless yuppie protagonist begins by grousing about a devastating earthquake that tragically interrupts *The Simpsons* and grows more and more psychotic until he's apoplectic that he ruined his knife by stabbing a co-worker.

Though Yankovic's singles invariably focus on easily recognizable mainstream fare, he never stopped being the accordion-playing kid whose world was rocked by Dr. Demento's cavalcade of craziness. *Poodle Hat* contains two of Al's most loving and elaborate homages. The head-spinningly conceptual "Bob" pays tribute to the poetic inscrutability of Bob Dylan with lyrics that sound cryptic enough to be genuinely Dylanesque but are in fact palindromes delivered in an uncanny re-creation of Dylan's nasal whine. "Genius in France" is even more ambitious—a nearly nine-

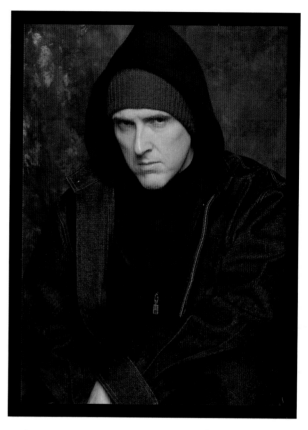

★ I spent hours practicing my glower for this Eminem-inspired promo shot.

minute-long cartoon epic in the style of Al's hero Frank Zappa that features a guitar solo by Frank's son Dweezil.

Eminem's refusal to allow a music video for "Couch Potato" had kneecapped *Poodle Hat*'s commercial chances. For Al, timeliness is of the utmost importance when it

  TWEET Me, trying to explain to my daughter what a jukebox was: "You know, kinda like an 800-lb. iPod."

comes to releasing singles. Wait too long and the cultural moment is gone. Al wasn't about to release something like "Party at the Leper Colony" (one of Al's periodic musical sacrifices to the god of bad taste) or "Genius in France" as a single, so Eminem's refusal left him in the lurch commercially and helped make *Poodle Hat* one of only three Weird Al albums never to go gold.

On April 9, 2004, tragedy darkened Yankovic's otherwise charmed life when his beloved parents, Nick and Mary, died of accidental carbon monoxide poisoning in their Fallbrook, California, home. As an only child, Yankovic was especially close to his parents, who took enormous pride in their son's accomplishments. Al, who was on tour at the time, was shocked and devastated by the news but performed that night as a form of therapy. As Yankovic told fans on a post that ran on his website, "I've heard from so many people over the years that my music has cheered them up in times of tragedy . . . well, I thought maybe my music would help me too."

In times of tragedy and hardship we need escapism and silliness and levity more than ever. Al found performing familiar songs in front of enthusiastic, empathetic crowds deeply cathartic and healing. Being able to share music and joy with audiences who loved him may not have made him forget the terrible tragedy that had befallen his parents (nothing could) but it helped him and his family make it through a painful period in their lives.

★ Friends, relatives, and paid extras are all featured on the cover of my *Poodle Hat* album. If you look closely, you can see the belly of my very pregnant wife (she was four days away from giving birth when this photo was taken). We tried taking the shot with everybody in the subway car at the same time, but ultimately decided to Photoshop their images individually.

★ This is our sweet poodle, Bela, who was immortalized on the *Poodle Hat* cover (and also provided a bark in my song "Genius in France"). We tried one setup where Bela was ostensibly urinating on my head, but ultimately decided it was more disgusting than funny.

★ When Mark Seliger tells me to jump, I ask, how high?

★ Jon "Bermuda" Schwartz (as Allen Ginsberg), yours truly (as Dylan), and Jay Levey (as Bob Neuwirth) in the "Subterranean Homesick Blues"–inspired video for my song "Bob" (shot as part of an *AL-TV* special).

ALBUQUERQUE

by AL YANKOVIC

Way back when I was just a little bitty boy living in a box under the stairs in the corner of the basement of the house half a block down the street from Jerry's Bait Shop . . . you know the place . . . well anyway, back then life was going swell and everything was juuuuust *peachy* . . . except of course for the undeniable fact that every single morning . . . my mother would make me a big ol' bowl of sauerkraut for breakfast . . . *Arggggh!* Big bowl of sauerkraut!! Every single morning!! It was driving me crazy! I said to my mom, I said, "Hey! Mom! What's up with all the sauerkraut??" And my dear sweet mother, she just looked at me like a cow looks at an oncoming train, and she leaned right down next to me, and she said, "Unhhhh . . . It's *goooood* for you!" And then she tied me to the wall and stuck a funnel in my mouth and force-fed me nothing but sauerkraut until I was twenty-six and a half years old. That's when I swore that someday, someday I would get out of that basement and travel to a magical, far-away place where the sun is always shining and the air smells like warm root beer and the towels are oh-so-fluffy . . . where the Shriners and the lepers play their ukuleles all day long and anyone on the street will gladly shave your back for a nickel. Wocka wocka doo doo yeah. Well, let me tell you, people, it wasn't long at all before my dream came true, because the very next day a local radio station had this contest to see who could correctly guess the number of molecules in Leonard Nimoy's butt. I was off by three, but I still won the grand prize . . . That's right, a first-class one-way ticket . . . to *Al . . . buquerque! Al . . . buquerque!* Oh yeah . . . You know, I'd never been on a real airplane before, and I gotta tell you, it was really great . . . except that I had to sit between two large Albanian women with excruciatingly severe body odor, and the little kid in back of me kept throwing up the whole time, and the flight attendants ran out of Dr Pepper and salted peanuts, and the in-flight movie was *Bio-Dome* with Pauly Shore, and three of the airplane engines burned out and we went into a tailspin and crashed into a hillside and the plane exploded in a giant fireball and everybody died . . . except for me . . . you know why? *'Cause I had my tray table up . . . and my seat back in the full upright position, had my tray table up . . . and my seat back in the full upright position . . . had my tray table up . . . and my seat back in the full upright position . . . Ha ha ha ha ha ha ha!!* So I crawled from the twisted, burning wreckage . . . I crawled on my hands and knees for three full days . . . dragging along my big leather suitcase and my garment bag and my tenor saxophone and my twelve-pound bowling ball and my lucky, lucky autographed glow-in-the-dark snorkel. But finally I arrived at the world-famous Albuquerque Holiday Inn where the towels are oh-so-fluffy . . . and you can eat your soup right out of the ashtrays if you wanna. It's okay, they're clean! Well, I checked into my room and I turned down the AC and I turned on the Spectravision and I'm just about to eat that little chocolate mint on my pillow that I love so very, very much when suddenly there's a knock on the door. Well, now who could that be? I say, "Who is it?" No answer. "Who is it?" There's no answer. "Who is it??" They're not sayin' anything. So finally I go over and I open the door, and just as I suspected . . . it's some big fat hermaphrodite with a Flock of Seagulls haircut and only one nostril. Ohhhh, man, I hate it when I'm right. So anyway, he bursts into my room and he grabs my lucky snorkel and I'm like, "Hey! You can't have that! That snorkel's been just like a snorkel to me!" And he's like, "Tough!" And I'm like, "Give it!" And he's like, "Make me!" And I'm like, "'kay!" So I grabbed his leg and he grabbed my esophagus and I bit off his ear and he chewed off my eyebrows and I took out his appendix and he gave me a colonic irrigation. Yes indeed, you better believe it. And somehow in the middle of it all the phone got knocked off the hook . . . and twenty seconds later, I heard a familiar voice, and you know what it said? I'll tell you what it said. It said, *"If you'd like to make a call, please hang up and try again. If you need help, hang up and then dial your operator . . . If you'd like to make a call, please hang up and try again. If you need help, hang up and then dial your operator...*" in *Al...buquerque! Al...buquerque!* Well, to cut a long story short, he got away with my snorkel. But I made a solemn vow right then and there that I would not rest... I would not sleep for an instant... until the one-nostriled man was brought to justice. But first I decided to buy some donuts. So I got in my car and I drove over to the donut shop and I walked on up to the guy behind the counter and he says, "Yeah, whaddaya want?" I said, "You got any glazed donuts?" He said, "No, we're outta glazed donuts." I said, "Well, you got any jelly donuts?" He said, "No, we're outta jelly donuts!" I said, "You got any Bavarian creme-filled donuts?" He said, "No, we're outta Bavarian creme-filled donuts!" I said, "You got any cinnamon rolls?" He said, "No, we're outta cinnamon rolls!" I said, "You got any apple fritters?" He said, "No, we're outta apple fritters!" I said, "You got any bear claws?" He said, "Wait a minute, I'll go check . . . . No!! We're outta bear claws!!" I said, "Well, in that case... in that case, what do you have?" He says, "All I got right now is this box of one dozen starving, crazed weasels." I said, "Okay. I'll take that." So he hands me the box and I open up the lid and the weasels jump out and they immediately latch onto my face and start biting me all over. *Arr arrrr arrrrh.* Oh man, they were just going nuts. They were tearing me apart! You know, I think it was just about that time that a little ditty started going through my head. I believe it went a little something like this: "*Arrrrrrgh!!! Get 'em off of me!!! Get 'em off me!!! Arggggggh!!! Get 'em off!! Get 'em off!! Arrrrrrrrgh... Arggggggggghh!!!*" I ran out into the street with these flesh-eating weasels all over my face, waving my arms all around and just running, running, running like a constipated wiener dog. And as luck would have it, that's exactly when I ran into the girl of my dreams. Her name was Zelda. She was a calligraphy enthusiast with a slight overbite and hair the color of strained peaches. I'll never forget the very first thing she said to me. She said, "Hey. You've got weasels on your face." That's when I knew it was true love. We were inseparable after that. Aw, we ate together, we bathed together, we even shared the same piece of mint-flavored dental floss. Aw, the world was our burrito. So we got married and we bought us a house and had two beautiful children, Nathaniel and Superfly. Oh, we were so very, very, very happy. Oh yeah. But then one fateful night, Zelda said to me, she said, "Sweetie Pumpkin... do you want to join the Columbia record club?" I said, "Whoa! Hold on now, baby! I'm just not ready for that kind of a commitment!" So we broke up and I never saw her again. But that's just the way things go... in *Al...buquerque! Al...buquerque!* Anyway, things really started looking up for me, because about a week later I finally achieved my life-long dream. That's right, I got me a part-time job at the Sizzler. I even made Employee of the Month after I put

out that grease fire with my face. Oh yeah, everybody was pretty jealous of me after that. I was gettin' a lot of *attitude.* Okay, like one time, I was out in the parking lot trying to remove my excess ear wax with a golf pencil, when I see this guy Marty trying to carry a big ol' sofa up the stairs all by himself. So I say to him, I say, "Hey! You want me to help you with that?" And Marty, he just rolls his eyes and goes, "Nooo, I want you to cut off my arms and legs with a chain saw." So I did. And then he gets all indignant on me! He's like, "Hey, man, I was just being sarcastic!" Well, that's just great. How was I supposed to know that? I'm not a mind-reader, for crying out loud. Besides, now he's got a really cute nickname—Torso Boy—so what's he complaining about? Say, that reminds me of another amusing anecdote. This guy comes up to me on the street and he tells me he hasn't had a bite in three days. Well, I knew what he meant, but just to be funny I took a big bite out of his jugular vein. And he's yelling and screaming and bleeding all over, and I'm like, "Hey! Come on! Don't you get it?" But he just keeps rolling around on the sidewalk, bleeding and screaming, "*Ahhhhh!! Ahhhhh!! Ahhhhhh!!!*"—y'know, completely missing the irony of the whole situation. Man, some people just can't take a joke, y'know? Anyway, I uh...um...where was I?......I kinda lost my train of thought. Uh... well, okay, anyway, I know it's kind of a round-about way of saying it, but I guess the whole point I'm trying to make here is... I... HATE... SAUERKRAUT!! That's all I'm really trying to say. And by the way, if one day you happen to wake up and find yourself in an existential quandary, full of loathing and self-doubt and wracked with the pain and isolation of your pitiful, meaningless existence, at least you can take a small bit of comfort in knowing that somewhere out there in this crazy ol' mixed-up universe of ours, there's still a little place... called *Al... buquerque! Al...buquerque! Albuquerque! Albuquerque! Albuquerque! Albuquerque!* I said, A! *(A!)* L! *(L!)* B! *(B!)* U! *(U!)* ... querque!! *(Querque!!)* Albuquerque! *(Albuquerque!)*

Albuquerque! *(Albuquerque!)*
Albuquerque! *(Albuquerque!)*
Albuquerque! *(Albuquerque!)*
Albuquerque! *(Albuquerque!)*
Albuquerque! *(Albuquerque!)*
Albuquerque! *(Albuquerque!)*
Albuquerque! *(Albuquerque!)*
Al . . . . . . buquerque!

CHAPTER 5

The ALPOCALYPSE APPROACHES

★ This is my disguise for whenever I want to go out in public incognito.

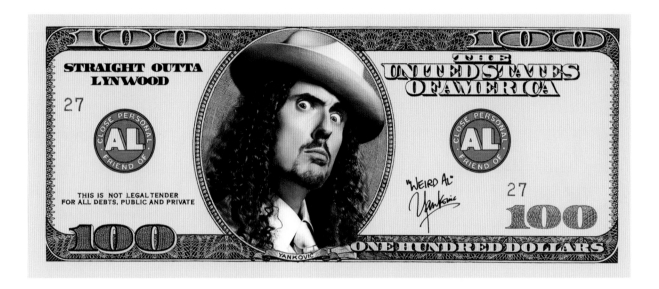

AS AL'S CAREER PROGRESSED, THE STAKES GREW HIGHER.

Al wasn't a goofy kid anymore. He was a middle-aged man with a family and a thriving career and a band and crew that depended on his continual creativity for their livelihood. Al was in it for the long haul, taking the long view. He understood that he'd be performing each new single hundreds of times in concert, and he didn't want to be saddled with a song he couldn't stand.

Al thought he'd found the perfect subject for his next spoof when he parodied painfully earnest young singer-songwriter James Blunt's breakout hit "You're Beautiful" as "You're Pitiful." Al received permission from Blunt, only to have Blunt's skittish label reject the parody on the basis it might harm James's fragile young career. The label had a commodity to protect; it wouldn't want a Weird Al parody to "destroy" Blunt's career the way Al's spoofs had previously "destroyed"

★ I Photoshopped and printed up a ton of this Al money to drop on audiences during our live performance of "I'll Sue Ya." Today they are worth . . . well, considerably less than face value.

the careers of Michael Jackson, Madonna, and Nirvana. Seriously, when was the last time you heard anybody talk about *them*?

Once again fate would intervene on Al's behalf and save him from making a mistake. "You're Pitiful," which Al leaked for fans as a free download before the full album was finished, was an amusing character study of the contemporary loser, but it was nowhere near as strong as the geek anthem that would become the first single off that album (2006's *Straight Outta Lynwood*) and, astonishingly, his biggest hit to date as a recording artist. Peaking at number nine, "White & Nerdy" was Yankovic's first top-ten pop hit ("Eat It" peaked at number twelve) as well as his first single to be certified platinum by the RIAA.

Al had again done the impossible. He'd scored his biggest hit twenty-seven

WHITE

& NERDY

Parody of "Ridin'" by CHAMILLIONAIRE
featuring KRAYZIE BONE

New lyrics by AL YANKOVIC

They see me mowin' . . . my front lawn
I know they're all thinkin' **I'm so white & nerdy**
Think I'm just too white & nerdy
Think I'm just too white & nerdy
Can't ya see I'm white & nerdy?
Look at me, I'm white & nerdy

I wanna roll with . . .
the gangstas

But so far they all think I'm too white & nerdy
Think I'm just too white & nerdy
Think I'm just too white & nerdy
I'm just too white & nerdy
Really, really white & nerdy

First in my class there at MIT
Got skills, **I'm a champion at D&D**
MC Escher, that's my favorite MC
Keep your 40, I'll just have an Earl Grey tea
My rims never spin—to the contrary

You'll find that they're quite stationary
All of my action figures are cherry

Stephen Hawking's in my library

My MySpace page is all totally pimped out
Got people beggin' for my Top 8 spaces
Yo, I know pi to a thousand places
Ain't got no grills, but **I still wear braces**
I order all of my sandwiches with mayonnaise
I'm a whiz at Minesweeper, I could play for days
Once you see my sweet moves, you're gonna stay amazed
My fingers movin' so fast, I'll set the place ablaze
There's no killer app I haven't run
At Pascal, well, I'm number one

Do vector calculus
JUST FOR FUN

I ain't got a gat but I got a soldering gun
"Happy Days" is my favorite theme song
I could sure kick your butt in a game of Ping-Pong
I'll ace any trivia quiz you bring on

I'm fluent in **JavaScript** as well as **Klingon**

Here's the part I sing on . . .

They see me roll on . . . my Segway
I know in my heart they think I'm white & nerdy
Think I'm just too white & nerdy
Think I'm just too white & nerdy
Can't ya see I'm white & nerdy?
Look at me, I'm white & nerdy
I'd like to roll with . . . the gangstas
Although it's apparent I'm too white & nerdy
Think I'm just too white & nerdy
Think I'm just too white & nerdy
I'm just too white & nerdy

How'd I get so white & nerdy?

I've been browsin', inspectin'
X-Men comics, you know I collect 'em

The pens in my pocket, I must protect 'em

My ergonomic keyboard never leaves me bored
Shoppin' online for deals on some writable media
I edit Wikipedia
I memorized *Holy Grail* really well
I can recite it right now and have you ROTFLOL
I got a business doin' web sites
When my friends need some code,
   who do they call?

I do HTML for 'em all
Even made a home page for my dog

Yo, I got myself a fanny pack

They were havin' a sale down at the Gap
Spend my nights with a roll of bubble wrap
Pop pop, hope no one sees me . . . gettin' freaky
I'm nerdy in the extreme and whiter than sour cream

I was in **A/V Club** and **Glee Club** and even the **chess team**

Only question I ever thought was hard
Was, do I like Kirk or do I like Picard?
Spend every weekend at the Renaissance Faire

Got my name on my underwear

They see me strollin' . . . they laughin'
And rollin' their eyes 'cause I'm so white & nerdy
Just because I'm white & nerdy
Just because I'm white & nerdy
All because I'm white & nerdy
Holy cow, I'm white & nerdy
I wanna bowl with . . . the gangstas
But oh well, it's obvious I'm white & nerdy
Think I'm just too white & nerdy
Think I'm just too white & nerdy
I'm just too white & nerdy

Look at me,
I'M WHITE & NERDY

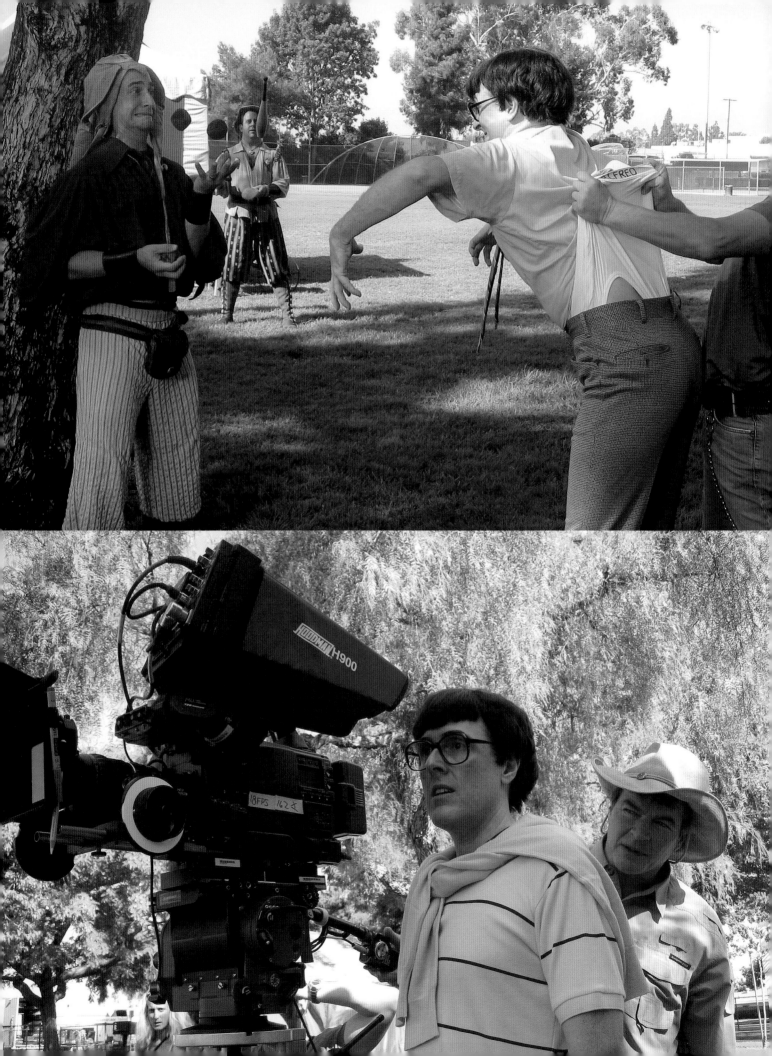

years into his career. Even more remarkably, he'd done it with a *rap* song from what was arguably his best album since *In 3-D*. "White & Nerdy" represented the apex of Yankovic's unlikely but fruitful flirtation with hip-hop.

"White & Nerdy" is the ultimate nerdcore anthem, a defiant howl of Poindexter pride. Al had evolved as an MC to the point where he could perfectly mimic Chamillionaire's machine-gun-fast, incredibly precise flow from "Ridin'" while remaining lucid and comprehensible and delivering a dense collage of pop-cultural references and jokes with perfect comic timing. As always with Al, there's real love and palpable affection behind the send-up of computer geekdom.

Al's musical *and* science-geek sides collided on "Pancreas," an insanely intricate homage to *Pet Sounds*–era Beach Boys as well as to the internal organ that gives the song's narrator nearly as much life-affirming joy as trips to the hardware store, cable TV, and a velvet Elvis painting gave the overenthusiasts in previous Weird Al songs.

Straight Outta Lynwood offers a master class on Al's favorite themes. Al's computer obsession informs the dazzling "Virus Alert," a pastiche in the style of Sparks about a sinister online entity that will, among other atrocities, "translate your documents into Swahili" and "make your TV record *Gigli*." And "Weasel Stomping Day" combines two of Al's most beloved tropes: a cheerful-sounding ditty about something disturbing (in this case, enthusiastic stomping of weasels by blood-crazed Weasel Stomping Day fans) and holidays as nightmarish vessels for humanity's worst instincts.

When they're not driven to heights of rapture by consumer goods and services, Al's overflowing gallery

★ I presented at the *American Music Awards* with Chamillionaire—I think he was impressed by my *gangsta stare*.

of oddball characters in his songs are driven to distraction by the mundane irritations of everyday life. The anger of the litigious lunatic behind the Rage Against the Machine–style "I'll Sue Ya" knows no bounds: he angrily demands justice in court for everything from fast food making him fat to Ben Affleck's existence, while the nitpicker of the Cake-inspired "Close But No Cigar" finds a reason to dump even a "world-famous billionaire bikini supermodel astrophysicist" for having one earlobe that was just a little bit too big.

  TWEET I love listening to early Beach Boys. Those are the kind of harmonies you can only get from YEARS of parental abuse.

★ "White & Nerdy" illustration by DKNG Studios

TWEET

I have to wonder what kind of names the band REJECTED before they settled on "Hoobastank."

FUN FACTS ABOUT CHARLES NELSON REILLY

Anytime CNR was feeling a sense of ennui, he would bite the head off a nearby penguin.

If you stared at Charles Nelson Reilly for more than twenty seconds, you would suffer permanent retinal damage.

CNR could hammer nails with his wrist, and once he brought a baby llama back from the dead.

CNR once dressed up like an astronaut for an entire year, and no one said a stinking word about it.

CNR was in the movie *French Connection*, but they cut him out 'cause he made Hackman look like a whiny little girl.

When it comes to blowing up minor irritations into major drama, nothing compares to "Trapped in the Drive-Thru." Al's job as a parodist entails making straightforward pop songs ridiculous, but it would have been impossible to make R. Kelly's "Trapped in the Closet" series more preposterous than it already was. So Al reversed his usual modus operandi: he made a ridiculous song mundane. He slyly robbed a melodramatic song of not only melodrama

★ Patton Oswalt and Thomas Lennon marvel at my commitment to craft after I shove a metal rod through my head to portray accident victim Phineas Gage in my short film *Al's Brain in 3-D*.

but also of any drama whatsoever. He retained the structure of "Trapped in the Closet" but turned it on its head so that the song relentlessly rushed toward the most mundane of climaxes—the delayed diner discovers that the burger joint forgot to put onions on his burger—instead of steering listeners through a series of unfortunate and wildly unlikely events à la Kelly.

Straight Outta Lynwood also saw Al take on the laughable self-righteousness of a recording industry that stops robbing artists blind only long enough to make earnest

★ Malcolm in the Middle! On the set of *Halloween II*
with Rob Zombie and Malcolm McDowell.

CNR

by AL YANKOVIC

Charles Nelson Reilly *was a mighty man*

The kind of man you'd never disrespect

He stood eight foot tall, wore glasses

And **he had a third nipple**
on the back of his neck

He ate his own weight in coal

And excreted diamonds every day

He could throw you down a flight of stairs

But you still would love him anyway

Yeah, you know you'd love him anyway

Charles Nelson Reilly won the Tour de France

With two flat tires and a missin' chain

He trained a rattlesnake to do his laundry

I'm tellin' you the man was insane

He could rip out your beatin' heart

And show it to you right before you died

Every day he'd make the host of Match Game
Give him a piggyback ride

Yeah, a two-hour piggyback ride

Giddyup, Gene!

Ninja warrior, master of disguise

He could melt your brain with his laser beam eyes

Oh yeah

Oh yeah

He had his very own line at the DMV

He made sweet, sweet love to a manatee

Oh yeah

Oh yeah, that was somethin' to see, I tell ya

Charles Nelson Reilly **sold his toenail clippings**
As a potent aphrodisiac

He ran a four-minute mile blindfolded

With an engine block strapped to his back

He could eat more frozen waffles

Than any other man I know

Once he fell off the Chrysler Building

And he barely even stubbed his toe

Had a tiny little scratch on his toe—didn't even hurt

Charles Nelson Reilly figured out cold fusion

But he never ever told a soul

I've seen the man unhinge his jaw

And swallow a Volkswagen whole

He'd bash your face in with a shovel
If you didn't treat him like a star

'Cause you can spit in the wind or tug on Superman's cape

But Lord knows you just don't mess around with CNR

No no no

Talkin' 'bout CNR

Ohh

PERMANENT ART

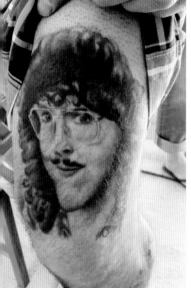

SOMEWHAT LESS PERMANENT
ART

★ After the release of *Straight Outta Lynwood*, I was invited to display my hometown pride by serving as the Grand Marshall in the Lynwood Christmas Parade.

The success of *Straight Outta Lynwood* heightened expectations for a follow-up. With each passing year, the pressure on Al mounted. A white forty-something accordion player had scored the biggest hit of his career with a rap song. It is a testament to the almost surreal eclecticism of Yankovic's oeuvre that this fact didn't strike many people as particularly strange.

In 2009 Sony released the *Internet Leaks* EP. As the title suggests, it was a compilation of tracks Al had released, or "leaked" digitally. The five-track EP was intended as a stopgap between *Straight Outta Lynwood* and his next proper studio album, but that didn't keep it from getting nominated for a Grammy for Best Comedy album all the same. The rise of iTunes and MP3s allowed Al to be timelier than ever: he was able to release his identically titled parody of hip-hop artist T.I.'s "Whatever You Like" while T.I.'s original was still number one on the charts.

But *Internet Leaks* would only satisfy fans for so long. Then Al would need the single that would launch his thirteenth studio album. He didn't just need the right hit to parody, he was patiently awaiting the arrival of a new icon that would rock the cultural zeitgeist the way Michael Jackson, Madonna, and Kurt Cobain had decades before. Another "Snack All Night" would not do. He could not rehash past triumphs. He needed something bold, something audacious, something new.

Within the context of Al's career, the stakes could not have been higher. He'd be performing the next single for the rest of his career, so it would be advantageous if he were able to listen to it repeatedly without wanting to take a chain saw to his cerebral cortex. "White & Nerdy" and *Straight Outta Lynwood* had over-performed in a

appeals to the public to stop taking food out of rock stars' mouths through file-sharing and music piracy on "Don't Download This Song." The song takes the form of a "We Are the World"–style power ballad, only instead of trying to raise money for starving children in Africa, it's about something really important: rooting out downloaders and treating them, in Al's indelible turn of phrase, like "the evil, hard-bitten criminal scum [they] are." To fuzzy things up even further, Al released his faux anti-downloading message song as . . . a free download.

  TWEET Wheeee! Look at me! I'm goin' 1,000 miles an hour!!! #rotationoftheeearth

★ I never had two-year-olds stop me at airports before until I
appeared as the Ringmaster on an episode of *Yo Gabba Gabba*.

"WEIRD AL" YANKOVIC

ALPOCALYPSE

★ This might be my favorite album cover ever.
Photo by the brilliant Robyn Von Swank.

music industry whose state at the time could charitably be called a hellish miasma of unrelenting horror hurtling madly toward oblivion. And things had only declined in the interim. Al has some of the most loyal, devoted, and obsessive fans in the business—if not *the* most loyal, devoted, and obsessive fans—but even some of the biggest names in history have struggled to sell albums in such an icy climate.

Al doggedly watched the pop charts and waited for the right cultural moment to strike. He'd need to hit it out of the park this time. "Good enough" would not be good enough. The fans were waiting. The record label was waiting. The band was waiting. Jon's garage full of Al memorabilia was waiting, and it was an inanimate object. Al's world was frozen in a state of intense, almost unbearable anticipation. Everything was riding on the next single.

Enter Lady Gaga.

The eccentric pop diva didn't just break out: she exploded into the stratosphere with an image, persona, and sound custom made for the Weird Al treatment. But Al couldn't launch what would be the most important album of his career with a parody of just any Lady Gaga single. He had to find the perfect one.

Then in 2011 Gaga released "Born This Way," and Al found his moment. "Born This Way" afforded Al an opportunity to lampoon not just the song but the artist, as he'd done with "Smells Like Nirvana." Even more remarkably, he would be able to parody Gaga and "Born This Way" in a manner that honored both the song's message of self-expression and the passionate artist behind it.

As always, Al asked the camp of the artist he was spoofing for permission to parody her hit. Al was a little reluctant to satirize a song with such an important social message, but he thought he had found a way to do so in a manner that was not only funny but also strangely respectful, even reverent.

When it comes to parodies, Al's band sets out to re-create the track they're parodying as closely as possible, so Al was understandably confused when Lady Gaga's representatives asked for not just Al's new lyrics but a recorded version of Al's parody. Nevertheless, Al

LAST WILL AND TESTAMENT

I'm not really sure what kind of funeral service I'd like. Surprise me.

Feel free to attach monofilament to my lips and eyelids for hilarious open-casket pranks!

I don't care what it says on my tombstone, as long as it's not in Comic Sans.

Please donate whatever money my family doesn't want to the ACTF (American Camel-Toe Foundation).

If possible, try to prevent *Variety* from using "Weird Al Eats It!" as their obit headline.

acquiesced. He and his band headed into the studio to record what Al had titled "Perform This Way" for the benefit of Gaga's management.

There was no reason for Gaga to feel anything but flattered by Al's parody, especially since he'd volunteered to donate his share of the single's proceeds to the Human Rights Campaign in honor of the Gaga anthem's message. Al was therefore sur-prised and disappointed when Lady Gaga's camp rejected the parody.

Even a man as cool-headed as Al must have experienced a moment of panic at the prospect of having to throw out the clever, timely, and insightful single he'd just written. Sure, the song took some affectionate jabs at Gaga's surrealistic sartorial sensibility, but it had done so in an affectionate and knowing manner.

★ It's a next-to-impossible task to one-up Lady Gaga, but we gave it our best shot. More than two dozen outfits were created for the music video, including this one, which featured an actual working model train going around the brim of a hat.

 TWEET

Oh, great. I just found out I'm arsenic-intolerant.

WEIRD AL YANKOVIC
July 17th Verizon Wireless Theater Houston, Texas

★ I believe this may be the first time I've ever directed a video in drag. Here I am calling the shots with my body double Vlada Gorbaneva and Madonna impersonator Holly Beavon.

Still, Lady Gaga's camp had said no. Al was flummoxed. On April 20, 2011, Al uploaded a "lyrics video" of the song on YouTube, accompanied by text explaining the situation. He also blogged on WeirdAl.com about Lady Gaga's representatives' refusal. This set off an explosive chain of events. In what appeared to be a staggering reversal, the Lady Gaga camp suddenly claimed that Lady Gaga herself had never heard the song and was a big Weird Al fan.

In an enormously satisfying and sane resolution to what was rapidly shaping up to be a pointless and migraine-inducing melodrama, Lady Gaga's manager admitted that he'd turned down the parody request on his artist's behalf without even consulting his client. Gaga then happily approved the parody, and the dark cloud that had been hanging over Al and the album and single he'd worked so hard on lifted.

★ Me, leaning against a Door. That's Ray Manzarek, legendary keyboard player for the Doors, who was kind enough to come into the studio and duplicate his signature sound for my song "Craigslist."

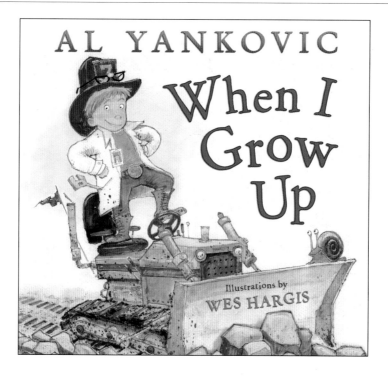

W

TWEET

"Don't put all your eggs in one basket" is propaganda from the American Council of Basket Makers.

Al had emerged triumphant. He was now free to express himself however he saw fit. He could now perform however he pleased. Al was now free to unleash his thirteenth album, *Alpocalypse*. As if all that weren't exciting enough, Lady Gaga told *Rolling Stone* that she found the parody "empowering" and called having Al parody her song a "rite of passage."

In the best Al tradition, "Perform This Way" is as much a celebration of Lady Gaga as it is a parody of her. Why wouldn't it be? Weird Al was promenading before the public in ridiculous get-

★ The cover of my first children's book. Never thought I'd be a *New York Times* best-selling author when *I* grew up!

ups before Lady Gaga was born. He'd been making a glorious spectacle of himself for more than three decades. The average Weird Al show might actually entail more costume changes and more outrageous looks than a Lady Gaga extravaganza.

Al had been hesitant about spoofing "Born This Way" precisely because he had such reverence for its message of tolerance and free expression. In its own peculiar way, "Perform This Way" echoes the original's liberating message: in Al's loving hands, it's a celebration of theatricality, of self-

TWEET

If I had a company that sold canned chicken, I would call it "Tuna Of The Land" . . . just to blow everyone's minds.

expression, and reinvention. Weird Al was celebrating Lady Gaga's constitutional right to dress and act like a male drag queen in performance despite being born a heterosexual woman as well as his own right to send up the ridiculousness of Gaga's gloriously excessive aesthetic.

The official OK had liberated Weird Al and his loyal band to do what they do best: travel the world spreading joy and laughter. It meant that Al was free to once again slip inside the skin and flamboyant stage costumes of a staggering array of pop icons and act out a funhouse-mirror version of the past three decades of pop culture in two eventful hours.

On *Alpocalypse,* the former architecture student creates dazzling new musical monuments out of

★ A supergroup is born: I got to rock out on stage with Alice Cooper and Steven Tyler for a benefit concert in Maui on New Year's Eve 2011.

the blueprints of pop music made by artists half Al's age. The parody "TMZ" based on Taylor Swift's "You Belong with Me" follows "Midnight Star" (from 1984's *"Weird Al" Yankovic in 3-D*) and "Jerry Springer" (from 1999's *Running With Scissors*) in spoofing the tawdry excesses of tabloid culture, while the Miley Cyrus parody "Party in the CIA" offers an inspired variation on an old Al staple: the upbeat-sounding song about something utterly dark and twisted. In this case, it's a CIA agent giddy about all the regime toppling, waterboarding, and mole-uncovering that lies in his immediate future.

As always, it's possible to chart the evolution of pop culture through Al's songs: the yuppie striving of "Buy Me a Condo" from

★ Between takes on the set
of *30 Rock* with Tina Fey.

In 3-D has long since given way to the recession-era economic anxiety of T.I.'s sugar-daddy anthem "Whatever You Like," subverting the original's crass consumerism with an irreverent ode to penny-pinching, while the exquisitely annoyed "Stop Forwarding That Crap to Me" and "Craigslist" (style parodies of Jim Steinman and the Doors, respectively) continue Al's ongoing explorations of the infinite irritants and attractions of the computer age.

Trends come and go. Technology changes. Pop culture evolves and changes. Through it all, Al abides.

Al never stops topping himself. And so thirty-two years after Capitol snuck "My Bologna" into stores on Christmas Eve, "Weird Al" Yankovic scored his highest-charting album ever when *Alpocalypse* debuted at number nine. The album at number eight? That would be Lady Gaga's *Born This Way*. Al's life and career have exceeded the bounds of even his own famously vivid imagination, but as *Alpocalypse*'s robust first week sales attest, the best could very well be yet to come. History has taught us it's foolish to underestimate Al.

Yankovic's unlikely but brilliant career is an enduring testament that a life spent wearing ridiculous costumes and singing crazy songs can be—and, in Al's case, most assuredly is—a life well spent.

DISCOGRAPHY

ALBUMS

"Weird Al" Yankovic
1983, Scotti Bros / Rock & Roll Records

"Weird Al" Yankovic in 3-D
1984, Scotti Bros / Rock & Roll Records

Dare to Be Stupid
1985, Scotti Bros / Rock & Roll Records

Polka Party!
1986, Scotti Bros / Rock & Roll Records

Even Worse
1988, Scotti Bros / Rock & Roll Records

UHF – Original Motion Picture Soundtrack and Other Stuff
1989, Scotti Bros / Rock & Roll Records

Off the Deep End
1992, Scotti Bros / Rock & Roll Records

Alapalooza
1993, Scotti Bros / Rock & Roll Records

Bad Hair Day
1996, Scotti Bros / Rock & Roll Records

Running with Scissors
1999, Volcano / Way Moby

Poodle Hat
2003, Volcano / Way Moby

Straight Outta Lynwood
2006, Volcano / Way Moby

Alpocalypse
2011, Volcano / Way Moby

COMPILATIONS AND SPECIAL RELEASES

"Weird Al" Yankovic's Greatest Hits
1988, Scotti Bros / Rock & Roll Records

Peter and the Wolf (with Wendy Carlos)
1988, CBS

The Food Album
1993, Scotti Bros / Rock & Roll Records

Permanent Record – Al in the Box
1994, Scotti Bros / Rock & Roll Records

Greatest Hits Volume II
1994, Scotti Bros / Rock & Roll Records

The TV Album
1995, Scotti Bros / Rock & Roll Records

Internet Leaks
2009, Volcano / Way Moby

The Essential "Weird Al" Yankovic
2009, Sony Legacy

The Essential
"Weird Al" Yankovic –
Limited Edition 3.0
2010, Sony Legacy

SINGLES (PRE-DIGITAL ERA)

"My Bologna"
b/w "School Cafeteria"
1979, Capitol Records

"Another One Rides the Bus" / "Happy Birthday"
b/w "Gotta Boogie" / "Mr. Frump in the Iron Lung"
1981, Placebo records

"Another One Rides the Bus"
b/w "Gotta Boogie"
1981, TK Records

"Ricky"
b/w "Buckingham Blues"
1983, Scotti Bros / Rock & Roll Records

"I Love Rocky Road"
b/w "Happy Birthday"
1983, Scotti Bros / Rock & Roll Records

"Eat It"
b/w "That Boy Could Dance"
1984, Scotti Bros / Rock & Roll Records

"I Lost on Jeopardy"
b/w "I'll Be Mellow When I'm Dead"
1984, Scotti Bros / Rock & Roll Records

"King of Suede"
b/w "Nature Trail to Hell"
1984, Scotti Bros / Rock & Roll Records

"This Is the Life"
b/w "Buy Me a Condo"
1984, Scotti Bros / Rock & Roll Records

"Like a Surgeon"
b/w "Slime Creatures from Outer Space"
1985, Scotti Bros / Rock & Roll Records

"I Want a New Duck"
b/w "Cable TV"
1985, Scotti Bros / Rock & Roll Records

"One More Minute"
b/w "Midnight Star"
1985, Scotti Bros / Rock & Roll Records

"Living with a Hernia"
b/w "Don't Wear Those Shoes"
1986, Scotti Bros / Rock & Roll Records

"Christmas at Ground Zero"
b/w "One of Those Days"
1986, Scotti Bros / Rock & Roll Records

"Fat"
b/w "You Make Me"
1988, Scotti Bros / Rock & Roll Records

"Lasagna"
b/w "Velvet Elvis"
1988, Scotti Bros / Rock & Roll Records

"I Think I'm a Clone Now"
b/w "(This Song's Just) Six Words Long"
1988, Scotti Bros / Rock & Roll Records

"UHF"
b/w "Attack of the Radioactive Hamsters from a Planet Near Mars"
1989, Scotti Bros / Rock & Roll Records

"Money for Nothing / Beverly Hillbillies"
b/w "Generic Blues"
1989, Scotti Bros / Rock & Roll Records

"Smells Like Nirvana"
b/w "Waffle King"
1992, Scotti Bros / Rock & Roll Records

"You Don't Love Me Anymore"
b/w "I Was Only Kidding"
1992, Scotti Bros / Rock & Roll Records

"Jurassic Park"
b/w "Frank's 2000 TV"
1993, Scotti Bros / Rock & Roll Records

"Bedrock Anthem"
b/w "Young, Dumb & Ugly"
1993, Scotti Bros / Rock & Roll Records

"Headline News"
b/w "Christmas at Ground Zero (Alternate Mix)"
1994, Scotti Bros / Rock & Roll Records

"Amish Paradise"
b/w "Everything You Know Is Wrong"
1996, Scotti Bros / Rock & Roll Records

"Amish Paradise"
b/w "Everything You Know Is Wrong" (plus bonus tracks)
1996, Scotti Bros / Rock & Roll Records

"Gump"
b/w "Spy Hard"
1996, Scotti Bros / Rock & Roll Records

"Gump"
b/w "Spy Hard" (plus bonus tracks)
1996, Scotti Bros / Rock & Roll Records

GRAMMY NOMINATIONS

"Eat It"
(Best Comedy Recording, 1984)
GRAMMY Award

Polka Party
(Best Comedy Recording, 1987)

Even Worse
(Best Comedy Recording, 1988)

"Fat"
(Best Concept Music Video, 1988)
GRAMMY Award

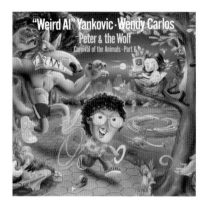

Peter and the Wolf
(Best Children's Recording, 1988)

Off the Deep End
(Best Comedy Recording 1992)

"Jurassic Park"
(Best Music Video, 1994)

Poodle Hat
(Best Comedy Album, 2003)
GRAMMY Award

Straight Outta Lynwood
(Best Comedy Album, 2006)

Straight Outta Lynwood
(Best Surround Sound Album, 2006)

Internet Leaks
(Best Comedy Album, 2009)

Alpocalypse
(Best Comedy Album, 2011)

"Perform This Way"
(Best Short Form Music Video, 2011)

VIDEOGRAPHY

MUSIC VIDEOS

"Ricky"
Parody of "Mickey" by Toni Basil
1983, directed by Janet Greek

"I Love Rocky Road"
Parody of "I Love Rock 'n' Roll"
by Joan Jett and the Blackhearts
1983, directed by Dror Soref

"Eat It"
Parody of "Beat It" by Michael Jackson
1984, directed by Jay Levey

"I Lost on Jeopardy"
Parody of "Jeopardy" by the Greg
Kihn Band
1984, directed by Jay Levey
and Robert K. Weiss

"This Is the Life"
1984, directed by Jay Levey
and Robert K. Weiss

"Like a Surgeon"
Parody of "Like a Virgin" by Madonna
1985, directed by Jay Levey
and Robert K. Weiss

"Dare to Be Stupid"
1985, directed by Jay Levey
and Robert K. Weiss

"One More Minute"
1985, directed by Jay Levey
and Robert K. Weiss

"Living with a Hernia"
Parody of "Living in America" by
James Brown
1986, directed by Jay Levey

"Christmas at Ground Zero"
1986, directed by Al Yankovic

"Fat"
Parody of "Bad" by Michael Jackson
1988, directed by Jay Levey

"Money for Nothing / Beverly Hillbillies"
Parody of "Money for Nothing" by
Dire Straits
1989, directed by Jay Levey

"UHF"
1989, directed by Jay Levey

"Smells Like Nirvana"
Parody of "Smells Like Teen Spirit"
by Nirvana
1992, directed by Jay Levey

"You Don't Love Me Anymore"
1992, directed by Jay Levey

"Jurassic Park"
Parody of "MacArthur Park" by
Richard Harris
1993, directed by Mark Osborne
and Scott Nordlund

"Bedrock Anthem"
Parody of "Under the Bridge" and
"Give It Away"
by Red Hot Chili Peppers
1993, directed by Al Yankovic

"Headline News"
Parody of "Mmm Mmm Mmm Mmm"
by Crash Test Dummies
1994, directed by Al Yankovic

"Amish Paradise"
Parody of "Gansta's Paradise" by
Coolio
1996, directed by Al Yankovic

"Gump"
Parody of "Lump" by the Presidents
of the United States of America
1996, directed by Al Yankovic

"Spy Hard"
1996, directed by Al Yankovic

"The Saga Begins"
Parody of "American Pie" by
Don McLean
1999, directed by Al Yankovic

"It's All About the Pentiums"
Parody of "It's All About the
Benjamins" by Puff Daddy
1999, directed by Al Yankovic

"Bob"
2003, directed by Al Yankovic

"Don't Download This Song"
2006, directed by Bill Plympton

"I'll Sue Ya"
2006, directed by Thomas Lee

"Virus Alert"
2006, directed by David C. Lovelace

"Close But No Cigar"
2006, directed by John Kricfalusi

"Pancreas"
2006, directed by Jim Blashfield

"Weasel Stomping Day"
2006, directed by Robot Chicken

"White & Nerdy"
Parody of "Ridin'" by Chamillionaire
2006, directed by Al Yankovic

"Do I Creep You Out"
Parody of "Do I Make You Proud" by
Taylor Hicks
2006, directed by JibJab

"Trapped in the Drive-Thru"
Parody of "Trapped in the Closet" by
R. Kelly
2007, directed by Doug Bresler

"Craigslist"
2009, directed by Liam Lynch

"Skipper Dan"
2009, directed by Divya Srinivasan

"CNR"
2009, directed by Jib-Jab

"Ringtone"
2009, directed by Josh Faure-Brac
and Dustin McLean

"Perform This Way"
Parody of "Born This Way" by
Lady Gaga
2011, directed by Al Yankovic

"Whatever You Like"
Parody of "Whatever You Like" by T.I.
2011, directed by Cris Shapan

"Party in the CIA"
Parody of "Party in the USA" by
Miley Cyrus
2011, directed by Roque Ballestros

"TMZ"
Parody of "You Belong with Me" by
Taylor Swift
2011, directed by Bill Plympton

"Another Tattoo"
Parody of "Nothin' On You" by B.o.B
featuring Bruno Mars
2011, directed by Augenblick Studios

"If That Isn't Love"
2011, directed by Brian Fisk

"Stop Forwarding That Crap to Me"
2011, directed by Koos Dekker

"Polka Face"
2011, directed by Melanie Mandl,
Wachtenheim/Marianetti, Philip Ed-
dolls, John Dilworth, Janet Perlman,
Sharon Colman, Anna Bermann, Dan
Meth, Chris Hinton, and Greg Holfeld

LONG-FORM VIDEOS

The Compleat Al
1985, CBS Fox

UHF
1990, Orion

"Weird Al" Yankovic Video Library
1992, Scotti Bros

"Weird Al" Yankovic: The Ultimate Collection
1993, Scotti Bros

Alapalooza: The Videos
1993, Scotti Bros

"Weird Al" Yankovic: The Videos
1997, Image

"Weird Al" Yankovic Live!
1999, Volcano / Way Moby

The Ultimate Video Collection
2003, Volcano / Way Moby

The Weird Al Show – The Complete Series
2006, Shout! Factory

"Weird Al" Yankovic Live! – The Alpocalypse Tour
2011, Paramount

Alpocalypse HD
2011, Volcano / Way Moby

PHOTO CREDITS

SONG LYRIC CREDITS